The Unauthorized Guide to OLYMPIC® PINS & MEMORABILIA

Jonathan Becker
& Gregory J. Gallacher

Schiffer® Publishing Ltd
4880 Lower Valley Road, Atglen, PA 19310 USA

Dedication

To all the talented athletes of the modern summer and winter games. Your dedication to your sport and courage on the playing fields is an inspiration to us all. Thank you for the memories! And to all Olympic memorabilia collectors, who are truly die-hard Olympic fans. Their interest and involvement has helped make the Olympic Games grow into one of the largest sporting events in the world.

Library of Congress Card Number: 2001095051

Designed by John P. Cheek
Cover design by Bruce M. Waters
Type set in Korinna BT/Korinna BT
ISBN: 0-7643-1491-2
Printed in China
1 2 3 4

Published by Schiffer Publishing Ltd.
4880 Lower Valley Road
Atglen, PA 19310
Phone: (610) 593-1777; Fax: (610) 593-2002
E-mail: Schifferbk@aol.com
Please visit our web site catalog at
www.schifferbooks.com
We are always looking for people to write books on new and related subjects. If you have an idea for a book please contact us at the above address.

This book may be purchased from the publisher.
Include $3.95 for shipping.
Please try your bookstore first.
You may write for a free catalog.

In Europe, Schiffer books are distributed by
Bushwood Books
6 Marksbury Ave.
Kew Gardens
Surrey TW9 4JF England
Phone: 44 (0) 20 8392-8585; Fax: 44 (0) 20 8392-9876
E-mail: Bushwd@aol.com
Free postage in the U.K., Europe; air mail at cost.

Contents

DARE TO DREAM
262 S. Main St.
saltlakepins.com
Pin Sales
Coca-Cola

Acknowledgments

We would like to thank the following people who have contributed their time, knowledge and expertise to make this book possible.

- Liz deFazio and the staff of the 1932 & 1980 Lake Placid Winter Olympic Museum
- Don Bigsby
- Dave Bushing
- Patricia Woodworth
- Karen Rosen

Introduction

In 1896, the Modern Olympic Games were re-established in Athens, Greece. Greece was a fitting site since the ancient Olympics had been held in Greece from 776 BC to 393 AD. Today the games are held every two years alternating between the summer and winter sports. The Olympics have now grown to monumental proportions. Television networks vie for the rights to broadcast these spectacles. Companies will spend millions to advertise their products on these telecasts. Cities around the world bid heavily for the honor and privilege to host the events. Billions are spent on venues to accommodate the sporting events, athletes, media, and spectators. Yes, the Olympic Games have evolved into a world showcase.

Sports, in general, create tremendous thrills, excitement, ecstasy, and disappointment. They provide images of greatness and failure. In no other sporting event is this more true then the Olympic Games.

Who can forget the human drama in the 1988 Winter Games in Calgary, Canada? American speed skater Dan Jansen at the top of his sport in the 1980's was expected to win numerous medals, just as did his American predecessor Eric Heiden did in the 1980 Lake Placid Winter Olympics. Tragedy struck as Dan's sister Jane passed away from Leukemia right before competition was to begin. Bravely, Dan competed in memory of his beloved sister. Possibly a lack of focus resulted in falling in the 500 meter race and four days later again in the 1000 meter. What an emotional moment!

Social issues are part of the Olympic spirit. In 1968 the plight of minorities and discrimination were brought to light at the Olympic games in Mexico City. African Americans Tommy Smith and John Carlos finish first and third respectively in the 200-meter track and field race. On the winners podium as the flag was raised and the national anthem played, their bowed heads and raised black-gloved fists created an unforgettable social statement.

Politics has also raised its sometimes-ugly head at the Olympics. Palestinian terrorists infiltrated the Olympic Village in Munich at the 1972 Summer Games and ultimately murdered 11 Israeli athletes. The cold war was in full force in the 1980's. Iran was holding American hostages. The Russian Army invaded Afghanistan. In the United States and much of the world, inflation was out of control. Americans were not feeling very good about themselves or their country. Teams of college students coached by Herb Brooks were to meet the Russian Olympic Hockey Team in Lake Placid, N.Y., at the 1980

Winter Olympics. The Russian Team was by far the best hockey team in the world. They beat the National Hockey League professional teams at almost every opportunity. It was said that the American kids had no chance and would be fortunate not to be embarrassed! "Do you believe in miracles?" This became the chant as these "kids" beat the World Champion Russian Team and went on to win the Olympic gold medal. The victory was voted the greatest sports moment of the 20th century. More importantly Americans felt a renewed pride in themselves and their country.

In reading and reviewing this book we hope to bring back some of the memories the Olympic Games evoke in you. We will take a look back at the torches used in the Olympic torch relays, the medals the athletes of the world unite together in competition to win, the pins and badges that are always a fan favorite at the Games, and so much more. Are they collectable? Do they have value? You will find out. Read on and have fun!

Collecting Olympic Memorabilia

If you are reading this book you are most likely interested in the Olympic games. You are probably also a collector of memorabilia, or at the least, considering becoming one. These are the questions commonly asked. Where would I find memorabilia to purchase? If need be will I be able to sell and how and where? How much should items cost? How much, if at all, does condition effect value? Let us explore these issues as it concerns the Olympic collector.

Where to Find Olympic Memorabilia

Sports and specifically Olympic memorabilia can be obtained or sold by various means.

•Flea markets/garage sales/antique shops: These avenues are the old guard of collecting. Although the search at these venues can be fun it is rarely rewarding. Olympic memorabilia just does not appear at these places anymore. This is not to say you can't pick up a trinket here or there. Just don't expect to be successful building a serious collection using this tactic. Sports and Olympic memorabilia have "dried up" here.

•Trade shows: There are numerous generic sports memorabilia and antique shows throughout the country every year. They include The "National Sports Convention" held annually in different U.S. cities, the huge antique show "Atlantique" held biannually in Atlantic City, and countless local shows held throughout the country. Olympic memorabilia shows up at these events on a limited basis. Baseball, football, basketball and hockey offerings will be more prevalent. You will be better served attending trade shows specific to the Olympics. A good example would be the annual Olympic pin and memorabilia festival held in picturesque Lake Placid, N.Y. each summer. While in Lake Placid be sure to visit the Lake Placid 1932 and 1980 Winter

Olympic Museum for a look back at the 1980 winter games and "The Miracle on Ice." In Switzerland, the Olympic Collectors World Fair is held semi-annually in Lausanne, at the International Olympic Committee Museum. This is a wonderful opportunity to view the museum and meet other collectors and enthusiasts while taking an international vacation. There are also Olympic pin and memorabilia shows held in conjunction with upcoming Olympic Games. These are usually held in or near the host cities.

•Sports memorabilia dealers will sell and buy Olympic memorabilia. Dealers can be found at trade shows mentioned in the last paragraph. You can subscribe to The Sports Collectors Digest commonly known as the SCD. Dealers advertise heavily in this weekly publication. To find local dealers just check your yellow pages or local newspaper. When selling, shop around your item, and make your best deal. Keep in mind that a dealer needs to resell your item at a mark-up to stay in business. Don't get frustrated if you don't get full retail value.

•Auctions are a fine source to buy and sell Olympic ware. There are numerous reputable auctions houses selling sports memorabilia including Olympic items. As baseball, football, basketball and hockey memorabilia begin to "dry up" or become recycled, Olympic memorabilia will become more prevalent. This trend is already beginning to take place. We are seeing more and more Olympic Game's "lots" being offered by the major sports auction houses every year. As with trade shows there are auctions specific to Olympic memorabilia. Again these auctions will yield the better opportunities to purchase your Olympic treasure.

•We live in a computer world. The Internet now has become the newest and the largest source for Olympic and sports memorabilia. "Ebay", for example, literally has thousands of Olympic pins and memorabilia for sale every week. The options to buy and sell are endless.

Flea markets, garage sales, antique shops, trade shows, auctions, the internet - they're all at your disposal to add to or liquidate your collection. A warning when buying. Always buy from a reputable source. Use this guide as a reference not just for value but also for authenticity. Remember buyer beware! Also buy within your means. Don't be a victim of "buyer regret." Follow those rules and enjoy your collection.

Condition and Values

Value is in the eye of the beholder. Value is a matter of supply and demand. Value is condition, condition, condition! All true but how do these adages pertain to Olympic memorabilia?

• Eye of the beholder: I like it therefore I'm going to buy it at any cost. I'm never going to sell it so I don't care what its worth. It is true liking an item is a key reason to buy. But maybe not at any cost. Remember there may come a time when you must sell your treasure. Also people's interests and taste in collecting change. By all means purchase your item but do keep resale value in mind.

• Supply vs. demand: Supply and demand can and will determine the value of a piece of memorabilia. Remember only the potential buyer and seller can determine the worth of a piece. If a collector needs a rare piece to complete a collection he or she may be willing to pay "top dollar." A unique piece will be of special interest to collectors. If there is only one known to exist how much is it worth? There is no real way to tell as it falls under the category of how badly a person or persons want the piece. Regional interests also affect the demand and, therefore, the value of merchandise. For example 1980 "Miracle on Ice" memorabilia will bring a premium to American Olympic and hockey collectors.

• Condition, condition, condition: Memorabilia in mint condition will sell at a premium. Unless unique, even a rare item will be a tough sell if it is in rough condition. Naturally, Olympic items from the 1904 St. Louis games cannot be expected to be in as good condition as an item from the 2000 Atlanta games. Take age into consideration but resist collecting "off grade" material. Many collectors will buy an "off grade" item as a filler to complete a set. The same collector will then look to "upgrade" by purchasing a better condition piece at a later date. This is fine but generally this collector will lose money on the transactions either because he bought retail and has to sell wholesale or he pays a buyer and sellers premium at auction. As a rule purchase the best condition piece you can afford and you will be a happier collector!

Remember this book is a guide. The seller and yourself will establish the value of the memorabilia for sale. Generally prices will rise in time and with inflation. There are exceptions, however. For example there may be a large find of an item in a warehouse or elsewhere. This will decrease the value of previously known pieces. If you are a collector don' t be overly concerned with the total "book value" of your collection. Display it, look at it, show it to your friends and enjoy it.

Displaying and Preserving Your Olympic Collection

The display and preservation of a collection is a prime consideration for the collector. Owning Olympic or sports memorabilia tucked away in safes or inaccessible space may be an investment but it's just no fun. You will enjoy your collection to its maximum if it is visually displayed.

Don't decorate... collect! Your collection can become beautiful accents to your home or office if done in good taste. Many antique collectors place their treasures among furnishings. Well, older Olympic memorabilia is just that - antique. A diploma from the 1912 Stockholm games in an antique frame would nicely compliment any wall. So would a torch from the 1936 Berlin games. Be creative and bring your collection to life!

There are display manufacturing companies that produce glass or Plexiglas fixtures, racks, and mannequins. These tend to be modern in appearance. You can add more charm and warmth to your exhibit with antique wooden display cabinets that are available for sale at flea markets and antique centers. Glass topped tables made of oak and other woods are available from numerous furniture manufacturers. You can opt to have custom-made displays manufactured for that special collection. This is a good idea for housing a specialty collection such as participation medals. The diameters and thicknesses of the medals vary. A professional cabinetmaker, or yourself if so inclined, could make an attractive and orderly display by making the proper size cutouts. An old trunk filled with Olympic equipment makes an attractive display. A collage of similar items in a shadow box makes for an organized display. Olympic pins can be displayed in this manner. They also display well on an Olympic souvenir hat or sweater. Others opt to display their pins and buttons in specially made cloth "pin books." Frame your Olympic diplomas and other paper souvenirs. Professional framing is a must. Be sure the image never touches the glass. Acid free matting and ultra violet glass should be used with any picture of value. The acid free matting will prevent chemical staining. The ultraviolet glass will keep harmful sunlight and artificial light from fading the images. Be bold! Show off your collection. You spent a lot of time and money in acquiring your treasures. Enjoy them!

Now that your collection is properly displayed. You are going to want to preserve and protect it to maintain its esthetic and financial value.

Light is an enemy of your collection. We talked about how to use ultraviolet glass on your picture framing to keep out damaging light. The rest of your items will need to be protected as well. Fabrics, printing, paint and photographs all fade. Paper goods will deteriorate more quickly when exposed to natural or artificial light. Avoid windows in your memorabilia room to keep out sunlight. If you have windows use blinds and keep them closed as often as possible. Window film can be purchased and applied to existing windows. You can install the film yourself or hire a professional. The window film will darken your room at varying degrees depending on the thickness. The thicker the film the less damaging light is emitted into the room. This may be an inconvenience, but it will do wonders to preserve your investment. Artificial light is also a problem. Do not shine lights directly on items that can fade. They will, and quickly. Try to keep all lights off except when necessary to view your collection or work in the memorabilia room. When light is absolutely necessary, indirect lighting is a key to preservation.

Other enemies the collector encounters are fingerprints, moths, and moisture. Avoid handling pieces. Oil from fingerprints can damage many items such as photographs and porous materials. Moths will raise havoc with woolen items you may have in display. Garment bags for uniforms will help, along with strategically placed pieces of cedar. There are also numerous other "gadgets" on the market to combat the dreaded moth. If dampness is a problem in your home use a dehumidifier to decrease the moisture. Moisture will create rust on metal, mildew on paper goods, and a damp odor on everything. Be prepared! Don't let these conditions and pests get established.

Care should be taken when dealing with fabric collectibles. Again, fabrics fade so avoid direct exposure to artificial light and sunlight. If you must wash items such as uniforms, avoid hot water. Wash in cold water only on the gentle cycle. Never assume an article is machine dryable. Bleach is to be avoided at all costs.

Fire is the master of destruction! It is difficult to combat this menace. I would avoid a water sprinkler system in a collectible room. If a sprinkler system should go off prematurely the damage would be great. Dry chemical systems are an alternative, albeit expensive. Many museums use this method to protect their collections. It may be the wise choice for a valuable collection. Fire alarm systems are a must throughout your home not just for the protection of your collection, but the safety of yourself and your family. Consider a system that can be centrally monitored so that the fire department and/or police can be summoned. Be careful, as caution is a key to fire prevention.

Protect against theft. Have a security system installed in your home. Again, consider a central station so that the police can respond quickly in case of a potential burglary. As we discussed earlier you will want to display your collection and show it to your friends and relatives. Do so, but also be aware that if you show your collection to everyone, someone may decide to make it their own. Use your discretion about who views your valuables.

Insuring your collection is strongly recommended. If the value exceeds your basic homeowners policy coverage, consider adding a rider to your homeowner's insurance. You will incur an added premium for this protection. You insure your home, car, jewelry, and other valuables. Why not your Olympic and sports collectibles? Keep an inventory of your collectibles along with their respective values. This will be a necessity if you insure your collections but should be done even if you don't. The inventory is easily listed on a computer and copies should be kept with your insurance company and in a safe or other secure place.

Displaying, preserving, and protecting your collection can be time-consuming and costly. However, the positives will far out way the negatives. Collect, enjoy and have piece of mind!

The Modern Olympic Games

SUMMER OLYMPIC GAMES

I	1896 Athens, Greece
II	1900 Paris, France
III	1904 St. Louis, USA
	1906 Athens – Intermediate (Olympic) Games
IV	1908 London, England
V	1912 Stockholm, Sweden
VI	1916 Berlin, Germany (canceled due to WWI)
VII	1920 Antwerp, Belgium
VIII	1924 Paris, France
IX	1928 Amsterdam, The Netherlands
X	1932 Los Angeles, USA
XI	1936 Berlin, Germany
XII	1940 Tokyo, Japan/Helsinki, Finland (canceled due to WWII)
XIII	1944 London, England (canceled due to WWII)
XIV	1948 London, England
XV	1952 Helsinki, Finland
XVI	1956 Melbourne, Australia (Equestrian events in Stockholm, Sweden)
XVII	1960 Rome, Italy
XVIII	1964 Tokyo, Japan
XIX	1968 Mexico City, Mexico
XX	1972 Munich, Germany
XXI	1976 Montreal, Canada
XXII	1980 Moscow, Soviet Union
XXIII	1984 Los Angeles, USA
XXIV	1988 Seoul, Korea
XXV	1992 Barcelona, Spain
XXVI	1996 Atlanta, USA
XXVII	2000 Sydney, Australia
XXVII	2004 Athens, Greece
XXVIII	2008 Beijing, China

WINTER OLYMPIC GAMES

I	1924 Chamonix, France
II	1928 St. Moritz, Switzerland
III	1932 Lake Placid, USA
IV	1936 Garmisch-Partenkirschen Germany
	1940 Sapporo, Japan/St. Moritz, Switzerland/ Garmisch-Partenkirchen, Germany (canceled due to WWII)
	1944 Cortina d'Ampezzo, Italy (canceled due to WWII)
V	1948 St. Moritz, Switzerland
VI	1952 Oslo, Norway
VII	1956 Cortina d'Ampezzo, Italy
VIII	1960 Squaw Valley, USA
IX	1964 Innsbruck, Austria
X	1968 Grenoble, France
XI	1972 Sapporo, Japan
XII	1976 Innsbruck, Austria
XIII	1980 Lake Placid, USA
XIV	1984 Sarajevo, Yugoslavia
XV	1988 Calgary, Canada
XVI	1992 Albertville, France
XVII	1994 Lillehammer, Norway
XVIII	1998 Nagano, Japan
XIX	2002 Salt Lake City, USA
XX	2006 Torino, Italy

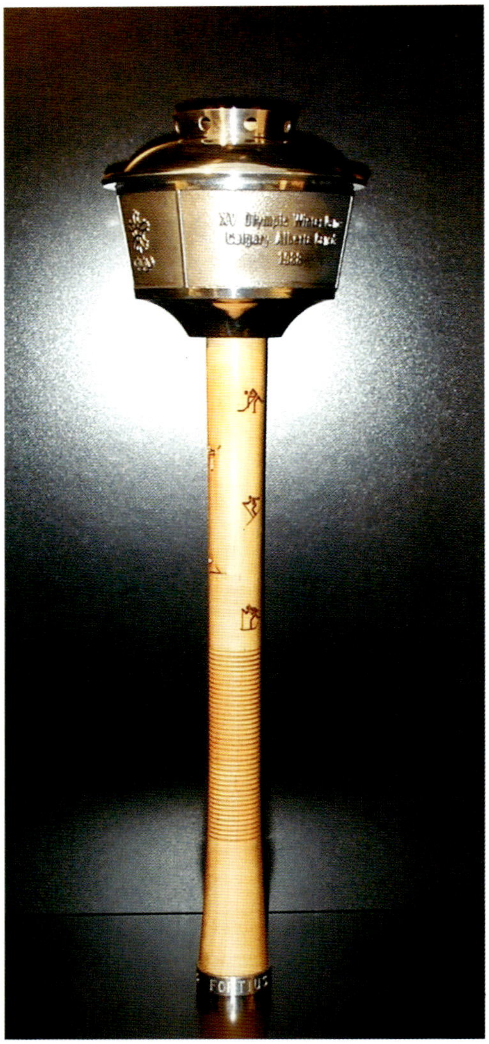

Rarity Scale

1 – Extremely rare or unique
2 – Rare
3 – Average availability
4 – Relatively common
5 – Plentiful

Please note: All collectibles are rated for rarity within their own category. For example: A "1" rarity prize medal may translate into only a dozen or so known to exist. Whereas, a "1" rarity mascot plush toy (although rare for a mascot) could mean there are hundreds available.

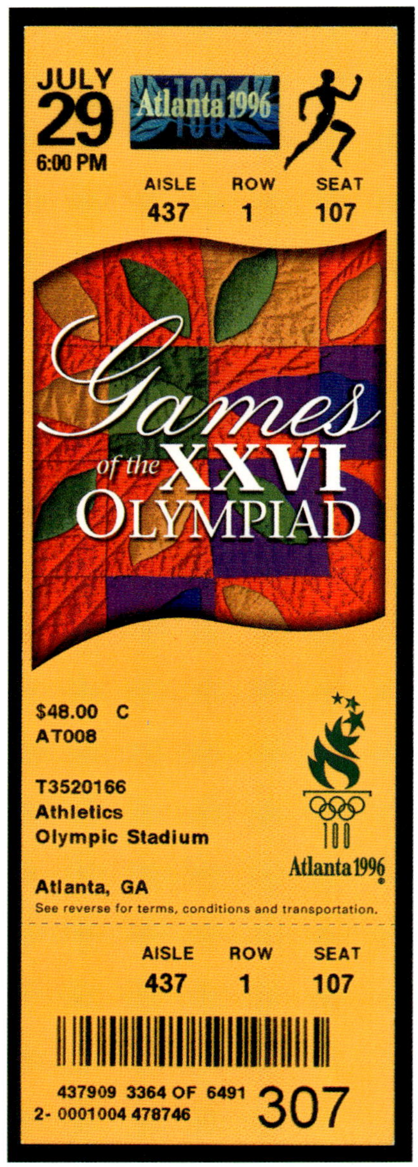

Olympic Pins

Pins are the most widely collected Olympic item. Many Olympic memorabilia collectors get their start with Olympic pins. Olympic pins had their origins as team badges that were traded among athletes and officials. The first team pins appeared in 1906 at the unofficial Athens Games. At subsequent Olympics more and more nations brought pins to the games. In 1912 the first souvenir Olympic pins were produced. The success of Olympic pin collecting and trading eventually brought about an explosion of pin types.

Today there are five main categories of Olympic pins. Olympic team pins include both dated and undated versions of pins produced by national Olympic committees, either for use by athletes and officials or for fund raising! In the 1960s two very popular forms of Olympic pins began to appear: media pins and sponsor pins. Media pins are those pins produced by broadcast, newspaper, and magazine organizations. Olympic sponsors who have paid substantial fees to Olympic organizations for commercial purposes produce sponsor pins. Mascot pins depict the official mascot of the games of that year. Finally, bid pins are produced by a prospective Olympic host city prior to being awarded an Olympic Games.

Olympic pins have grown from only a handful in the early years of the Olympic movement to the thousands that are available today. Traditionally the pins that have retained their value or increased in value are team pins, media pins, and mascot pins. We have chosen to focus on those types in this chapter. Due to the huge number of Olympic pins available, this price guide gives a sampling of pins and pin types from each Olympics.

GRADING OLYMPIC PINS

Olympic pins, especially older examples, can vary widely in condition. Many times the original collector put them in a box or bag and the pins became scratched and chipped. It is important to look for smooth surfaces, compete backs, and even coloring. As with many collectibles, it is better to wait for a pin in excellent condition than choose one that is so-so. Down the line the better pins will retain their value.

Average condition: Slight wear to high relief points. Possible tiny rim nicks. No major problems.

Near mint condition: Out of the box quality. No visible naked eye flaws.

RARITY SCALE

See page 12

Year	City	Description	Rarity	Avg.	N. Mint
1904	St. Louis	Enameled brass flag with legend	4	$75	$100
1904	St. Louis	Tin flag with "St. Louis 1904"	4	$65	$85
1904	St. Louis	Celluloid flag on a pin with advertisement on back	4	$50	$75
1904	St. Louis	Enameled brass pin in the shape of the Louisiana Purchase with legend	4	$75	$100
1904	St. Louis	Enameled round brass pin with fleur-de-lis, "St. Louis 1904," button attachment on back	4	$75	$100
1904	St. Louis	Celluloid button with expo logo	4	$75	$100
1904	St. Louis	Souvenir pin with "St. Louis 1904" over hanging colored glass	4	$100	$125
1904	St. Louis	Large enameled broach with exposition logo in center	3	$150	$200

1904, St. Louis. Large enameled broach with exposition logo in center, $150-200.

1904, St. Louis. Celluloid flag on a pin with advertisement on back, $50-75.

1904, St. Louis. Souvenir pin with "St. Louis 1904" over hanging colored glass, $100-125.

1904, St. Louis. Celluloid button with expo logo, $75-100.

1904, St. Louis. Enameled round brass pin with fleur-de-lis, "St. Louis 1904," $75-100.

1904, St. Louis. Enameled brass pin in the shape of the Louisiana Purchase, $75-100.

1904, St. Louis. Enameled brass flag, $75-100.

1904, St. Louis. Tin flag with "St. Louis 1904", $65-85.

Year	City	Description	Rarity	Avg.	N. Mint
1908	London	Czechoslovakia team pin	2	$250	$300
1912	Stockholm	Official souvenir stick pin in silver	3	$125	$150
1912	Stockholm	IOC Participation pin in white plastic wallet (distribution began in the 1980s & 1990s)	2	$125	$150
1912	Stockholm	Czechoslovakia team pin	2	$200	$225
1920	Antwerp	IOC Participation pin	2	$100	$125
1920	Antwerp	Sweden team pin	2	$200	$250
1924	Chamonix	IOC Participation pin	2	$125	$150
1924	Paris	City of Paris souvenir pin	2	$125	$150
1924	Paris	Switzerland team pin	2	$175	$200
1924	Paris	Sweden team pin	2	$175	$200
1924	Paris	IOC Participation pin	3	$75	$100
1928	Amsterdam	IOC Participation pin	3	$50	$75
1928	Amsterdam	Czechoslovakia fencing team pin	3	$100	$125
1928	Amsterdam	Czechoslovakia team pin	2	$150	$175

1912, Stockholm. Official souvenir stick pin in silver, $125-150.

1908, London. Czechoslovakia team pin, $250-300.

1920, Antwerp. Sweden team pin, $200-250.

1912, Stockholm. Czechoslovakia team pin, $200-225.

1924, Paris. City of Paris pin, $125-150.

1924, Paris. Switzerland team pin, $175-200.

1928, Amsterdam. Czechoslovakia fencing team pin, $100-125.

1924, Paris. Sweden team pin, $175-200.

1928, Amsterdam. Czechoslovakia team pin, $150-175.

Year	City	Description	Rarity	Avg.	N. Mint
1928	Amsterdam	IOC Winner's pin: gold-silver-bronze in black plastic wallet (distribution began in the 1980s & 1990s)	2	$150	$175
1928	Amsterdam	French team pin	2	$175	$200
1928	St. Moritz	IOC Participation pin	3	$50	$75
1928	St. Moritz	IOC Winner's pin	2	$175	$200
1928	St. Moritz /Amsterdam	Round silver colored pin with Olympic in center and legend around edge	4	$100	$125
1932	Lake Placid	IOC Participation pin	2	$100	$125
1932	Lake Placid	IOC Winner's pin	2	$175	$200
1932	Los Angeles	Sweden team pin	3	$125	$150
1932	Los Angeles	IOC Participation pin	3	$50	$65
1932	Los Angeles	Small US souvenir pin	4	$50	$75
1932	Los Angeles	Denmark team pin	4	$50	$75
1932	Los Angeles	IOC Winner's pin	3	$125	$150
1936	Berlin	Czechoslovakia team pin	3	$100	$125
1936	Berlin	Souvenir pin of Olympic bell	4	$40	$60

1928, St. Moritz/Amsterdam. Round silver colored pin with Olympic rings in center and legend around edge, $100-125.

1928, Amsterdam. IOC Participation pin, $50-75.

1932, Los Angeles. Sweden team pin, $125-150.

1932 Los Angeles. Denmark team pin, $50-75.

1936, Berlin. Czechoslovakia team pin (version 2), $100-125.

1932. Los Angeles. Small US souvenir pin, $50-75.

1936, Berlin. Souvenir pin of Olympic bell, $40-60.

Year	City	Description	Rarity	Avg.	N. Mint
1936	Berlin	Official souvenir pin of Brandenburg Gate	4	$40	$60
1936	Berlin	Czechoslovakia team pin (version 2)	3	$100	$125
1936	Berlin	Hungary team pin with ribbon	2	$400	$450
1936	Berlin	Turkey team pin	3	$150	$175
1936	Berlin	IOC Winner's pin	3	$125	$150
1936	Berlin	Portugal team pin	2	$375	$400
1936	Berlin	Canada team pin	3	$100	$125
1936	Berlin	IOC Participation pin	3	$50	$65

1936, Berlin. Portugal team pin, $375-400.

1936, Berlin. Hungary team pin with ribbon, $400-450.

1936, Berlin. Official souvenir pin of Brandenburg Gate, $40-60.

1936, Berlin. Turkey team pin, $150-175.

1936, Berlin. Canada team pin, $100-125.

1936, Berlin. Czechoslovakia team pin, $100-125.

Year	City	Description	Rarity	Avg.	N. Mint
1936	Garmisch	IOC Participation pin	3	$65	$75
1936	Garmisch	Official souvenir pin	4	$50	$75
1936	Garmisch	Souvenir pin with edelweiss over legend and Olympic rings	4	$60	$75
1936	Garmisch	IOC Winner's pin	2	$150	$175
1936	Garmisch	Official souvenir pin (version 2)	4	$75	$100
1940	Helsinki	Brass souvenir pin with Olympic flame on top over Olympic rings and legend	3	$150	$175
1940	Helsinki	Official logo pin	4	$50	$75
1940	Helsinki	Souvenir pin with Olympic rings	3	$150	$175
1948	London	Republic of China team pin	3	$100	$125

1936, Garmisch. Souvenir pin with edelweiss over legend and Olympic rings, $60-75.

1936, Garmisch. Official souvenir pin, $50-75.

1936, Garmisch. Official souvenir pin (version 2), $75-100.

1940, Helsinki. Official logo pin, $50-75.

1940, Helsinki. Souvenir pin with Olympic rings, $150-175.

1948, London. Silver plated brass official logo pin, $40-60.

1940, Helsinki. Brass souvenir pin with Olympic flame on top over Olympic rings and legend, $150-175.

1948, London. Republic of China team pin, $100-125.

Year	City	Description	Rarity	Avg.	N. Mint
1948	London	Switzerland team pin	3	$75	$100
1948	London	Silver plated brass official logo pin	4	$40	$60
1948	London	IOC Participation pin	3	$50	$65
1948	London	IOC Winner's pin	3	$80	$100
1948	London	Korea team pin	3	$75	$100
1948	London	Puerto Rico team pin	3	$50	$65
1948	St. Moritz	IOC Participation pin	3	$65	$75
1948	St. Moritz	IOC Winner's pin	3	$100	$125
1948	St. Moritz	Official logo pin	3	$75	$100
1948	St. Moritz	Austria team pin	2	$200	$250
1952	Helsinki	Great Britain Team pin	3	$150	$175

1948, London. Korea team pin, $75-100.

1948, London. Switzerland team pin, $75-100.

1948, London. Puerto Rico team pin, $50-65.

1952, Helsinki. Austria team pin, $100-125.

1948, St. Moritz. Official logo pin, $75-100.

1948, St. Moritz. Austria team pin, $200-250.

1952, Helsinki. Great Britain Team pin, $150-175.

Year	City	Description	Rarity	Avg.	N. Mint
1952	Helsinki	Austria team pin	3	$100	$125
1952	Helsinki	Switzerland team pin	3	$75	$100
1952	Helsinki	IOC Participation pin	4	$45	$55
1952	Helsinki	IOC Winner's pin	3	$75	$85
1952	Helsinki	Official logo pin	4	$35	$45
1952	Oslo	IOC Participation pin	3	$55	$65
1952	Oslo	IOC Winner's pin	3	$90	$100
1952	Oslo	Official logo pin	4	$75	$85
1952	Oslo	Austria team pin	2	$450	$500
1956	Cortina	Austria team pin	3	$250	$300
1956	Cortina	IOC Winner's pin	3	$90	$100
1956	Cortina	United States team pin	3	$75	$100
1956	Cortina	IOC Participation pin	3	$55	$65
1956	Melbourne	Visitor pin	4	$35	$45
1956	Melbourne	India team pin	3	$100	$125
1956	Melbourne	IOC Winner's pin	3	$65	$75
1956	Melbourne	Souvenir pin with kangaroo over rings	4	$15	$20
1956	Melbourne	Official logo pin	4	$35	$50
1956	Melbourne	Thailand team pin	3	$125	$150
1956	Melbourne	IOC Participation pin	4	$45	$55
1956	Melbourne	Austria team pin	3	$125	$150

1952, Helsinki. Official logo pin, $35-45.

1952, Helsinki. Switzerland team pin, $75-100.

1952, Oslo. Official logo pin, $75-85.

1956, Cortina. Austria team pin, $250-300.

1956, Melbourne. Souvenir pin with kangaroo over rings, $15-20.

1956, Cortina. United States team pin, $75-100.

1956, Melbourne. Austria team pin, $125-150.

Year	City	Description	Rarity	Avg.	N. Mint
1956	Melbourne	France team pin	3	$150	$175
1956	Melbourne	Great Britain team pin	3	$150	$175
1956	Stockholm	IOC Participation pin	2	$125	$150
1956	Stockholm	Official logo pin	4	$45	$60
1956	Stockholm	IOC Winner's pin	2	$150	$175
1960	Rome	Malaya team pin	3	$100	$125
1960	Rome	IOC Participation pin	4	$40	$50
1960	Rome	Netherlands team pin	3	$75	$100
1960	Rome	West Indies team pin	3	$100	$125

1956, Melbourne. Great Britain team pin, $150-175.

1956, Melbourne. Thailand team pin, $125-150.

1956, Melbourne. France team pin, $150-175.

1956, Melbourne. Visitor pin, $35-45.

1956, Stockholm. Official logo pin, $45-60.

1956, Melbourne. India team pin, $100-125.

1960, Rome. West Indies team pin, $100-125.

Year	City	Description	Rarity	Avg.	N. Mint
1960	Rome	Afghanistan team pin	3	$75	$100
1960	Rome	Official souvenir pin (version 2)	4	$35	$45
1960	Rome	Puerto Rico team pin	3	$75	$100
1960	Rome	Official souvenir pin (version 1)	4	$25	$35
1960	Rome	IOC Winner's pin	3	$60	$70
1960	Rome	Venezuela team pin	2	$135	$150
1960	Squaw Valley	Souvenir pin	4	$50	$60

1960, Rome. Venezuela team pin, $135-150.

1960, Rome. Netherlands team pin, $75-100.

1960, Rome. Malaya team pin, $100-125.

1960, Rome. Afghanistan team pin, $75-100.

1960, Rome. Official souvenir pin (version 1), $25-35.

1960, Rome. Official souvenir pin (version 2), $35-45.

1960, Rome. Puerto Rico team pin, $75-100.

1960, Squaw Valley. Souvenir pin, $50-60.

Year	City	Description	Rarity	Avg.	N. Mint
1960	Squaw Valley	Official logo pin (cutout version)	4	$75	$100
1960	Squaw Valley	Official logo pin (non cutout version)	4	$75	$100
1960	Squaw Valley	IOC Winner's pin	3	$80	$90
1960	Squaw Valley	IOC Participation pin	3	$55	$65
1960	Squaw Valley	Austria team pin	3	$150	$175
1960	Squaw Valley	Japan team pin	3	$125	$150
1960	Squaw Valley	Small curved rectangular pin with games logo and legend around edge, "Pageantry" at bottom	3	$150	$175
1964	Innsbruck	IOC Winner's pin	3	$70	$80
1964	Innsbruck	Official logo pin (small size)	4	$25	$30
1964	Innsbruck	Official logo pin (large size)	4	$35	$40
1964	Innsbruck	ABC Television pin	2	$175	$200
1964	Innsbruck	IOC Participation pin	3	$45	$55
1964	Tokyo	IOC Winner's pin	3	$60	$70
1964	Tokyo	IOC Participation pin	4	$40	$50
1964	Tokyo	UER EBU media pin	3	$180	$200
1964	Tokyo	Mongolia team pin	3	$85	$100
1964	Tokyo	Official logo pin	4	$35	$45
1968	Grenoble	Czechoslovakia team pin	4	$35	$45
1968	Grenoble	Official logo pin (small size)	4	$35	$50
1968	Grenoble	IOC Winner's pin	3	$70	$80
1968	Grenoble	Official logo pin (large size)	4	$55	$65
1968	Grenoble	ABC Television pin	3	$100	$125
1968	Grenoble	IOC Participation pin	3	$40	$50
1968	Mexico City	IOC Participation pin	4	$35	$45
1968	Mexico City	BBC Television pin	2	$275	$300
1968	Mexico City	ABC Television pin	3	$75	$100
1968	Mexico City	Official logo pin	4	$25	$30
1968	Mexico City	IOC Winner's pin	3	$60	$70
1972	Munich	IOC Participation pin	4	$35	$45
1972	Munich	ABC Television pin	3	$75	$100
1972	Munich	IOC Winner's pin	3	$55	$65
1972	Munich	ABC Television guest badge	3	$150	$175
1972	Munich	Philippines team pin	3	$50	$75

1960, Squaw Valley. Austria team pin, $150-175.

1960, Squaw Valley. Official logo pin (non cutout version), $75-100.

1960, Squaw Valley. Small pin with games logo and legend around edge, "Pageantry" at bottom, $150-175.

1964, Innsbruck. Official logo pin (large size), $35-40.

1972, Munich. ABC Television pin, $75-100.

1968, Grenoble. Czechoslovakia team pin, $35-45.

1968, Grenoble. Official logo pin (large size), $55-65.

1972, Munich. Philippines team pin, $50-75.

Year	City	Description	Rarity	Avg.	N. Mint
1972	Munich	Egypt team pin	4	$50	$65
1972	Munich	West Germany team pin	4	$30	$35
1972	Munich	Official logo pin	5	$20	$25
1972	Munich	BBC Television pin	3	$100	$125
1972	Munich	Japan team pin	4	$50	$65
1972	Munich	Khmer Republic (Cambodia) team pin	2	$225	$250
1972	Munich	Korea team pin	4	$50	$65

1972, Munich. West Germany team pin, $30-35.

1972, Munich. Egypt team pin, $50-65.

1972, Munich. Official logo pin, $20-25.

1972, Munich. BBC Television pin, $100-125.

1972, Munich. Khmer Republic (Cambodia) team pin, $225-250.

1972, Munich. Japan team pin, $50-65.

1972, Munich. Korea team pin, $50-65.

Year	City	Description	Rarity	Avg.	N. Mint
1972	Sapporo	Czechoslovakia team pin (stick pin)	4	$25	$30
1972	Sapporo	Official logo pin	4	$35	$45
1972	Sapporo	Czechoslovakia team pin (clutch back)	4	$35	$45
1972	Sapporo	IOC Participation pin	3	$40	$50
1972	Sapporo	IOC Winner's pin	3	$70	$80
1976	Innsbruck	Official logo pin	5	$15	$20
1976	Innsbruck	"Schneemann" mascot pin	4	$25	$30
1976	Innsbruck	United States team pin	4	$35	$50
1976	Innsbruck	IOC Winner's pin	3	$65	$75
1976	Innsbruck	IOC Participation pin	3	$40	$50
1976	Innsbruck	ABC Television pin	3	$75	$100
1976	Montreal	Sudan team pin	3	$35	$50
1976	Montreal	Taiwan team pin	3	$40	$50
1976	Montreal	Colombia team pin	3	$50	$70
1976	Montreal	IOC Participation pin	4	$35	$45
1976	Montreal	ABC Television pin	3	$75	$100
1976	Montreal	"Amik" mascot pin	4	$25	$30
1976	Montreal	BBC Television pin	3	$75	$100
1976	Montreal	TV + Radio Europe pin	3	$50	$70
1976	Montreal	Official logo pin	5	$15	$20
1976	Montreal	Mexico team pin	3	$45	$55

1976, Innsbruck. "Schneemann" mascot pin, $25-30.

1976, Innsbruck. ABC Television pin, $75-100.

1972, Sapporo. Czechoslovakia team pin (stick pin), $25-30.

1972, Sapporo. Czechoslovakia team pin (clutch back), $35-45.

1976, Montreal. Sudan team pin, $35-50.

1976, Montreal. Taiwan team pin, $40-50.

1976, Montreal. TV + Radio Europe pin, $50-70.

1976, Montreal. Colombia team pin, $50-70.

1976, Montreal. Mexico team pin, $45-55.

1976, Montreal. BBC Television pin, $75-100.

Year	City	Description	Rarity	Avg.	N. Mint
1976	Montreal	IOC Winner's pin	3	$55	$65
1976	Montreal	Soviet Union team pin	3	$25	$35
1976	Montreal	Jamaica team pin	3	$50	$70
1980	Lake Placid	ARZ-ZDF Radio-TV pin	4	$40	$50
1980	Lake Placid	Taiwan team pin	3	$45	$60
1980	Lake Placid	Austria team pin	4	$35	$45
1980	Lake Placid	Korea team pin	4	$25	$35
1980	Lake Placid	Czechoslovakia team pin (large size)	4	$25	$35
1980	Lake Placid	Daily Olympic Digest pin	3	$150	$175

1976, Montreal. Soviet Union team pin, $25-35.

1980, Lake Placid. ARZ-ZDF Radio-TV pin, $40-50.

1976, Montreal. Jamaica team pin, $50-70.

1980, Lake Placid. Taiwan team pin, $45-60.

1980, Lake Placid. Austria team pin, $35-45.

1980, Lake Placid. Czechoslovakia team pin (large size), $25-35.

1980, Lake Placid. Korea team pin, $25-35.

1980, Lake Placid. Daily Olympic Digest pin, $150-175.

Year	City	Description	Rarity	Avg.	N. Mint
1980	Lake Placid	BBC Television pin	3	$175	$200
1980	Lake Placid	"Roni" mascot pin (round)	5	$10	$12
1980	Lake Placid	ABC Television pin	4	$35	$45
1980	Lake Placid	"Roni" mascot pin (cutout)	5	$10	$12
1980	Lake Placid	Sports Illustrated pin	4	$25	$30
1980	Lake Placid	IOC Participation pin	3	$50	$60
1980	Lake Placid	IOC Winner's pin	3	$70	$80
1980	Lake Placid	ABC Television guest badge	3	$75	$100
1980	Lake Placid	Souvenir official logo pin	5	$15	$20
1980	Moscow	Puerto Rico team pin	4	$25	$35
1980	Moscow	West Germany team pin	4	$25	$30
1980	Moscow	BBC Television	3	$50	$70
1980	Moscow	NBC Television pin	3	$40	$50
1980	Moscow	Portugal team pin	4	$25	$35
1980	Moscow	"Mischa" mascot pin (cutout)	5	$5	$6
1980	Moscow	IOC Participation pin	4	$35	$40
1980	Moscow	"Mischa" mascot pin (round)	5	$5	$6
1980	Moscow	Official logo pin	5	$10	$15

1980, Lake Placid. "Roni" mascot pin (cutout), $10-12.

1980, Lake Placid. BBC Television pin, $175-200.

1980, Lake Placid. Sports Illustrated pin, $25-30.

1980, Lake Placid. ABC Television guest badge, $75-100.

1980, Moscow. BBC Television, $50-70.

1980, Moscow. "Mischa" mascot pin (round), $5-6.

1980, Lake Placid. Souvenir official logo pin, $15-20.

1980, Moscow. NBC Television pin, $40-50.

Year	City	Description	Rarity	Avg.	N. Mint
1980	Moscow	IOC Winner's pin	4	$55	$65
1984	Los Angeles	ABC Television pin	5	$15	$20
1984	Los Angeles	United States team pin set	3	$225	$275
1984	Los Angeles	IOC Participation pin	4	$30	$35
1984	Los Angeles	ABC Television guest badge	4	$30	$40
1984	Los Angeles	United States team pin	4	$20	$25
1984	Los Angeles	West Germany team	4	$15	$20
1984	Los Angeles	IOC Winner's pin	4	$50	$60
1984	Los Angeles	"RAI" Italian radio & television pin	3	$80	$100
1984	Los Angeles	Egypt team pin	4	$20	$30
1984	Los Angeles	"Sam" mascot pin	5	$5	$6
1984	Los Angeles	Bulgaria team pin	5	$10	$15
1984	Los Angeles	Official logo pin	5	$10	$15
1984	Los Angeles	Bolivia team pin	4	$35	$50
1984	Los Angeles	Portugal team pin	4	$25	$35
1984	Los Angeles	Mexico team pin	4	$20	$30
1984	Los Angeles	Thailand team pin	4	$50	$75

1980, Moscow. "Mischa" mascot pin (cutout), $5-6.

1980, Moscow. West Germany team pin, $25-30.

1984, Los Angeles. Bolivia team pin, $35-50.

1984, Los Angeles. ABC Television pin, $15-20.

1984, Los Angeles. United States team pin, $20-25.

1984, Los Angeles. ABC Television guest badge, $30-40.

1984, Los Angeles. Thailand team pin, $50-75.

1984, Los Angeles. Bulgaria team pin, $10-15.

1984, Los Angeles. West Germany team, $15-20.

1984, Los Angeles. Portugal team pin, $25-35.

1984, Los Angeles. Mexico team pin, $20-30.

Year	City	Description	Rarity	Avg.	N. Mint
1984	Sarajevo	Bulgaria team pin	4	$15	$20
1984	Sarajevo	IOC Participation pin	3	$45	$55
1984	Sarajevo	Opening ceremonies pin	4	$15	$20
1984	Sarajevo	Official logo pin	5	$10	$12
1984	Sarajevo	United States team pin set	2	$250	$300
1984	Sarajevo	Sports Illustrated pin	4	$30	$40

1984, Los Angeles. Egypt team pin, $20-30.

1984, Sarajevo. Opening ceremonies pin, $15-20.

1984, Sarajevo. Sports Illustrated pin, $30-40.

1984, Sarajevo. Official logo pin, $10-12.

1984, Sarajevo. Bulgaria team pin, $15-20.

Year	City	Description	Rarity	Avg.	N. Mint
1984	Sarajevo	Lake Placid-Sarajevo flight pin	3	$20	$25
1984	Sarajevo	"Vucko" mascot pin	4	$15	$18
1984	Sarajevo	ABC Television pin	4	$20	$25
1984	Sarajevo	BBC Television pin	3	$50	$65
1984	Sarajevo	IOC Winner's pin	3	$65	$75
1984	Sarajevo	United States team pin	4	$20	$25
1984	Sarajevo	ABC Television guest badge	4	$40	$50
1988	Calgary	United States team pin	4	$15	$20
1988	Calgary	United States team pin set	4	$175	$200
1988	Calgary	ABC Television pin	5	$10	$15
1988	Calgary	IOC Participation pin	3	$40	$45
1988	Calgary	San Marino team pin	4	$35	$45
1988	Calgary	Soviet team pin (large, generic type)	4	$25	$35
1988	Calgary	"Hidy and Howdy" mascot pin	4	$10	$12
1988	Calgary	Romania team pin	4	$20	$25
1988	Calgary	Czechoslovakia team pin	4	$15	$20
1988	Calgary	CTV (Canadian Television) pin	4	$15	$20

1984, Sarajevo. ABC Television guest badge, $40-50.

1984, Sarajevo. United States team pin set, $250-300.

1984, Sarajevo. BBC Television pin, $50-65.

1984, Sarajevo. "Vucko" mascot pin, $15-18.

1984, Sarajevo. ABC Television pin, $20-25.

1988, Calgary. CTV (Canadian Television) pin, $15-20.

Year	City	Description	Rarity	Avg.	N. Mint
1988	Calgary	Official logo pin-enameled	5	$10	$12
1988	Calgary	Official logo pin-non enameled	5	$10	$12
1988	Calgary	Great Britain team pin	4	$50	$60
1988	Calgary	Sweden team pin	4	$35	$50
1988	Calgary	IOC Winner's pin	4	$60	$70
1988	Calgary	Soviet Union team pin (individual sport)	4	$25	$30
1988	Calgary	Virgin Islands team pin	4	$35	$45

1988, Calgary. Romania team pin, $20-25.

1988, Calgary. ABC Television pin, $10-15.

1988, Calgary. Virgin Islands team pin, $35-45.

1988, Calgary. Official logo pin-non enameled, $10-12.

1988, Calgary. Czechoslovakia team pin, $15-20.

1988, Calgary. San Marino team pin, $35-45.

1988, Calgary. Official logo pin-enameled, $10-12.

Year	City	Description	Rarity	Avg.	N. Mint
1988	Seoul	Malaysia team pin	4	$10	$15
1988	Seoul	NHK Television pin	4	$45	$55
1988	Seoul	United States team pin set	4	$175	$225
1988	Seoul	IOC Winner's pin	4	$50	$60
1988	Seoul	Korean Broadcasting System (KBS)	4	$45	$55
1988	Seoul	"Hodori" mascot pin	4	$10	$15
1988	Seoul	United States team pin	4	$10	$15
1988	Seoul	IOC Participation pin	4	$30	$35
1988	Seoul	Switzerland team pin	3	$85	$100
1988	Seoul	BBC Television pin	4	$65	$75
1988	Seoul	NBC Television pin (undated)	4	$10	$15
1988	Seoul	Qatar team pin	4	$35	$45
1988	Seoul	Argentina team pin	4	$25	$30

1988, Calgary. Soviet team pin (large, generic type), $25-35.

1988, Seoul. BBC Television pin, $65-75.

1988, Calgary. Sweden team pin, $35-50.

1988, Seoul. Malaysia team pin, $10-15.

1988, Seoul. "Hodori" mascot pin, $10-15.

1988, Seoul. Canada team pin, $20-25.

1988, Seoul. Qatar team pin, $35-45.

1988, Seoul. Argentina team pin, $25-30.

Year	City	Description	Rarity	Avg.	N. Mint
1988	Seoul	Pakistan team pin	4	$30	$40
1988	Seoul	Canada team pin	4	$20	$25
1988	Seoul	Zimbabwe team pin	4	$35	$45
1988	Seoul	Jamaica team pin	4	$45	$55
1992	Albertville	United States team pin set	4	$150	$200
1992	Albertville	Taiwan team pin	4	$20	$25
1992	Albertville	United States team pin	4	$15	$20
1992	Albertville	IOC Participation pin	4	$30	$35
1992	Albertville	Bulgaria team pin	4	$15	$20
1992	Albertville	Korea team pin	4	$20	$25
1992	Albertville	Canada team pin	4	$15	$20
1992	Albertville	"Magique" mascot pin	4	$15	$20
1992	Albertville	CBS Television pin	4	$15	$20
1992	Albertville	IOC Winner's pin	4	$60	$70
1992	Albertville	Official logo pin	4	$20	$25
1992	Albertville	CBS Television guest badge	4	$35	$45
1992	Albertville	Czechoslovakia team pin	4	$15	$20

1988, Seoul. Pakistan team pin, $30-40.

1988, Seoul. Jamaica team pin, $45-55.

1988, Seoul. Korean Broadcasting System (KBS), $45-55.

1988, Seoul. Zimbabwe team pin, $35-45.

1988, Seoul. NHK Television pin, $45-55.

1992, Albertville. Taiwan team pin, $20-25.

1992, Albertville. Bulgaria team pin, $15-20.

1992, Albertville. Czechoslovakia team pin, $15-20.

Year	City	Description	Rarity	Avg.	N. Mint
1992	Barcelona	Malaysia team pin	4	$15	$20
1992	Barcelona	Taiwan team pin	4	$10	$15
1992	Barcelona	United States team pin	4	$10	$15
1992	Barcelona	Czechoslovakia team pin	4	$10	$15
1992	Barcelona	German Radio-TV pin (ARD-ZDF)	4	$15	$20
1992	Barcelona	Sports Illustrated pin	4	$15	$20
1992	Barcelona	United States team pin set	4	$200	$225
1992	Barcelona	NBC Television pin	5	$15	$20

1992, Albertville. Canada team pin, $15-20.

1992, Barcelona. Malaysia team pin, $15-20.

1992, Albertville. United States team pin set, $150-200.

1992, Barcelona. Sports Illustrated pin, $15-20.

1992, Albertville. Korea team pin, $20-25.

Year	City	Description	Rarity	Avg.	N. Mint
1992	Barcelona	Official logo pin	5	$8	$10
1992	Barcelona	Germany team pin	4	$15	$20
1992	Barcelona	BBC Television pin	4	$45	$55
1992	Barcelona	"Cobi" mascot pin (cutout)	4	$10	$15
1992	Barcelona	IOC Winner's pin	4	$50	$60
1992	Barcelona	NBC Radio affiliate pin	4	$15	$20
1992	Barcelona	IOC Participation pin	5	$20	$25
1992	Barcelona	NBC Television guest badge	4	$35	$45
1994	Lillehammer	United States team pin set	5	$125	$150
1994	Lillehammer	"Haakon and Kristin" mascot pin	4	$10	$15
1994	Lillehammer	TNT Television U.S. hockey pin	4	$20	$25

1992, Barcelona. BBC Television pin, $45-55.

1992, Barcelona. NBC Television pin, $15-20.

1992, Barcelona. NBC Radio affiliate pin, $15-20.

1992, Barcelona. Czechoslovakia team pin, $10-15.

1992, Barcelona. Official logo pin, $8-10.

1992, Barcelona. Germany team pin, $15-20.

1992, Barcelona. Taiwan team pin, $10-15.

1992, Barcelona. "Cobi" mascot pin (cutout), $10-15.

1992, Barcelona. German Radio-TV pin (ARD-ZDF), $15-20.

1994, Lillehammer. USA souvenir pin with legend, $15-20.

1994, Lillehammer. Sport pin, $10-15.

1994, Lillehammer. TNT Television U.S. hockey pin, $20-25.

Year	City	Description	Rarity	Avg.	N. Mint
1994	Lillehammer	CTV (Canadian Television) pin	4	$10	$15
1994	Lillehammer	Canada Team pin	4	$20	$25
1994	Lillehammer	CBS Television pin	4	$20	$25
1994	Lillehammer	IOC Winner's pin	4	$60	$70
1994	Lillehammer	USA souvenir pin with legend	4	$15	$20
1994	Lillehammer	CBS Television guest badge	4	$35	$45
1994	Lillehammer	IOC Participation pin	4	$30	$35
1994	Lillehammer	United States team pin	4	$10	$15
1994	Lillehammer	Sport pin	4	$10	$15
1994	Lillehammer	Slovenja team pin	4	$15	$20
1994	Lillehammer	Germany team pin	4	$10	$15
1996	Atlanta	Peru team pin	4	$10	$15
1996	Atlanta	"Izzy" mascot pin	5	$5	$6
1996	Atlanta	Sports Illustrated photo pin	4	$20	$25
1996	Atlanta	Kenya team pin	4	$25	$35
1996	Atlanta	United States team pin	4	$10	$15
1996	Atlanta	Official logo pin	5	$5	$7
1996	Atlanta	IOC Winner's pin	4	$50	$60
1996	Atlanta	Asahi Television pin	3	$90	$100
1996	Atlanta	"Olympic Report" radio pin	4	$15	$20
1996	Atlanta	IOC Participation pin	5	$20	$25
1996	Atlanta	SRC Sports pin	4	$15	$20
1996	Atlanta	NBC Television guest badge	4	$40	$50
1996	Atlanta	United States team pin set	5	$175	$200
1996	Atlanta	Israel team pin	4	$10	$15
1996	Atlanta	NBC Television pin	5	$10	$12
1996	Atlanta	Comores team pin	4	$45	$55
1996	Atlanta	Slovakia team pin	4	$10	$15
1996	Atlanta	Taiwan team pin	4	$10	$15
1996	Atlanta	Mexico team pin	4	$15	$20
1996	Atlanta	Belarus team pin	4	$15	$20
1996	Atlanta	Colombia team pin	4	$20	$25

1994, Lillehammer. United States team pin set, $125-150.

1994, Lillehammer. Germany team pin, $10-15.

1994, Lillehammer. CBS Television pin, $20-25.

1994, Lillehammer. CTV (Canadian Television) pin, $10-15.

1994, Lillehammer. Slovenja team pin, $15-20.

1996, Atlanta. Belarus team pin, $15-20.

1996, Atlanta. Mexico team pin, $15-20.

1996, Atlanta. NBC Television pin, $10-12.

1996, Atlanta. Colombia team pin, $20-25.

1996, Atlanta. Kenya team pin, $25-35.

1996, Atlanta. Sports Illustrated photo pin, $20-25.

1996, Atlanta. SRC Sports pin, $15-20.

1996, Atlanta. Israel team pin, $10-15.

1996, Atlanta. Taiwan team pin, $10-15.

1996, Atlanta. Comores team pin, $45-55.

1996, Atlanta. Slovakia team pin, $10-15.

1996, Atlanta. Peru team pin, $10-15.

1996, Atlanta. "Olympic Report" radio pin, $15-20.

Year	City	Description	Rarity	Avg.	N. Mint
1998	Nagano	Latvia team pin	4	$10	$15
1998	Nagano	United States team pin set	4	$175	$200
1998	Nagano	IOC Winner's pin	4	$60	$70
1998	Nagano	Germany team pin	5	$10	$15
1998	Nagano	IOC Participation pin	4	$25	$30
1998	Nagano	Switzerland team pin	4	$20	$25
1998	Nagano	CBS Television guest badge	4	$40	$50
1998	Nagano	"Snowlets" mascot pin	5	$5	$6
1998	Nagano	Georgia team pin	4	$10	$15
1998	Nagano	Brasil team pin	4	$15	$20
1998	Nagano	Official logo pin	5	$5	$7
1998	Nagano	CBS Television pin	5	$10	$12
1998	Nagano	United States team pin	4	$10	$15
1998	Nagano	Denmark team pin	4	$20	$25
1998	Nagano	Italy team pin	4	$15	$20
1998	Nagano	Liechtenstein team pin	4	$10	$15

1998, Nagano. Slovakia team pin, $225-225.

1998, Nagano. Latvia team pin, $10-15.

1998, Nagano. Netherlands team pin, $10-15.

1998, Nagano. Georgia team pin, $10-15.

1998, Nagano. Liechtenstein team pin, $10-15.

Year	City	Description	Rarity	Avg.	N. Mint
1998	Nagano	Netherlands team pin	4	$10	$15
1998	Nagano	Czech Republic team pin	4	$15	$20
1998	Nagano	Slovakia team pin	3	$225	$250

1998, Nagano. Italy team pin, $15-20.

1998, Nagano. Germany team pin, $10-15.

1998, Nagano. Denmark team pin, $20-25.

1998, Nagano. United States team pin, $10-15.

1998, Nagano. Switzerland team pin, $20-25

1998, Nagano. Czech Republic team pin, $15-20.

1998, Nagano. Brasil team pin, $15-20.

Year	City	Description	Rarity	Avg.	N. Mint
2000	Sydney	Namibia team pin	4	$20	$25
2000	Sydney	IOC Winner's pin	4	$50	$60
2000	Sydney	Official logo pin	5	$5	$6
2000	Sydney	IOC Participation pin	5	$15	$20
2000	Sydney	Yemen team pin	3	$90	$100
2000	Sydney	"Ollie, Syd, and Millie" mascot pin	5	$5	$6
2000	Sydney	NBC Television pin (no date)	5	$5	$7
2000	Sydney	Slovenja team pin	4	$20	$25
2000	Sydney	Taiwan team pin	4	$15	$20
2000	Sydney	Sports Illustrated pin	5	$15	$20
2000	Sydney	United States team pin	4	$10	$15
2000	Sydney	Time Magazine pin	5	$10	$15
2000	Sydney	German Television pin	4	$25	$35
2000	Sydney	NBC Television guest badge	4	$45	$55
2000	Sydney	Peru team pin	4	$15	$20

2000, Sydney. Peru team pin, $15-20.

2000, Sydney. German Television pin, $25-35.

2000, Sydney. Slovenja team pin, $20-25.

2000, Sydney. Namibia team pin, $20-25.

2000, Sydney. NBC Television guest badge, $45-55.

2000, Sydney. Taiwan team pin, $15-20.

2000, Sydney. Time Magazine pin, $10-15.

2000, Sydney. Sports Illustrated pin, $15-20.

Olympic Badges

Before the advent of plastic identification cards that are so common today, badges were used as identification for individuals in sports and special events. At the first Olympic Games in 1896 athletes and officials were identified by the type of paper badges attached to a shirt or jacket by a small ribbon. In 1904 officials wore a medal and ribbon on their coat or shirt. Throughout the years the types and numbers of badges grew to encompass virtually every official job involved in an Olympic Games. During the 1970s security became a prime consideration in identifying Olympic participants. Badges had become purely decorative and expensive to produce. Expenses were increasing and revenues declining. These factors led to badges becoming officially discontinued by the 1980 games. Many of the badges used at Olympic Games (especially earlier badges) are intricate works of art with beautiful detailing and vibrant colors. Some of the earliest badges are among the rarest of Olympic memorabilia. Many are quite large measuring as large as 150mm or more in length (including a ribbon).

GRADING OLYMPIC BADGES

Olympic badges can vary widely in condition. Many are struck in metal and then covered in fine cloisonné or enamel. Over the years heavy wear can result especially to enamel. Most of the earlier badges were made to higher standards than the most recent ones. This was usually due to the huge growth in Olympic participation. As quantities needed to be increased costs had to be cut and quality suffered.

Average condition: Slight wear to high relief points. Possible tiny rim nicks. No major problems.

Near mint condition: Out of the box quality. No visible naked eye flaws.

1904, St. Louis. Official (crossed oars "NAAO", rowing events), $6000-7000.

RARITY SCALE

See page 12. Another consideration in the rarity of badges is variations in color or ribbons. In many Olympic Games the ribbon had text that identified the sport or official capacity of the bearer. In other Olympics colors on the badges themselves identified sport and capacity.

Year	City	Description	Rarity	Avg	Nr Mint
1896	Athens	Paper badge with ribbon	1	$3000	$3500
1900	Paris	Jury badge, Universal Exposition	3	$1500	$1800
1904	St. Louis	Official (participation medal w/ribbon)	1	$12000	$16000
1904	St. Louis	Official (crossed oars "NAAO", rowing events)	1	$6000	$7000
1906	Athens	Athlete's badge	2	$650	$700
1908	London	"Referee"	2	$2300	$2400
1908	London	"Competitor"	3	$600	$700
1908	London	"Steward Committee"	2	$3000	$3100
1908	London	"Steward"	2	$1500	$1700
1908	London	"Judge"	2	$1400	$1500
1908	London	"Score-Keeper"	2	$1500	$1600
1908	London	"For services rendered"	2	$3300	$3500
1908	London	"Polytechnic committee"	2	$3300	$3500
1908	London	"Gymnastics"	1	$2000	$2200

1908, London. "Competitor", $600-700.

1906. Athens. Athlete's badge, $650-700.

1908, London. "Polytechnic Committee", $3300-3500.

1908, London. "Committee", $3000-3100.

Year	City	Description	Rarity	Avg	Nr Mint
1912	Stockholm	Competitor	3	$225	$300
1912	Stockholm	Official's badge (with ribbons)	2	$1000	$1100
1920	Antwerp	Competitor	1	$2000	$2200
1924	Chamonix	"Presse"	2	$3000	$3200
1924	Chamonix	"Officiel"	2	$3000	$3200
1924	Chamonix	"Concurrent" (athlete)	2	$3000	$3200
1924	Paris	"Presse"	3	$325	$350
1924	Paris	"Concurrent" (with ribbon)	2	$750	$800
1924	Paris	"Officiel" (with ribbon)	2	$2800	$2000
1924	Paris	"Concurrent"	3	$225	$275
1924	Paris	"Officiel" (official)	3	$275	$300

1912, Stockholm. Official's badge (with ribbons), $1000-1100.

1912, Stockholm. Competitor, $225-300.

1924, Chamonix. "Concurrent" (athlete), $3000-3200.

1924, Chamonix. "Officiel", $3000-3200.

1924, Paris. "Concurrent", $225-275.

1924, Chamonix. "Presse", $3000-3200.

1924, Paris. "Officiel" (official), $275-300.

1924, Paris. "Presse", $325-350.

1928, Amsterdam. "Presse", $250-300.

Year	City	Description	Rarity	Avg	Nr Mint
1928	Amsterdam	"Concurrent" (with ribbon)	3	$1100	$1200
1928	Amsterdam	"Officiel" (with rosette)	2	$1100	$1150
1928	Amsterdam	"C.I.O." (International Olympic Committee)	2	$1500	$1700
1928	Amsterdam	"Presse"	3	$250	$300
1928	Amsterdam	"C.I.O." (with ribbon)	1	$2000	$2200
1928	St. Moritz	"Presse"	3	$650	$700
1928	St. Moritz	"Concurrent"	3	$650	$700
1928	St. Moritz	"Officiel"	3	$650	$700
1928	St. Moritz	"C.I.O."	2	$800	$850
1932	Lake Placid	"Official"	2	$2500	$2800
1932	Lake Placid	"Honor Guest" (with ribbon)	1	$2700	$3000
1932	Lake Placid	"NY State OWG Comm" (with ribbon)	1	$2700	$3000
1932	Lake Placid	"III OWG Committee" (with ribbon)	2	$2500	$2700
1932	Lake Placid	"Official" (with ribbon)	2	$2500	$2700
1932	Lake Placid	"I.O.C."	1	$3000	$3200
1932	Lake Placid	"Contestant"	2	$2500	$2800
1932	Lake Placid	"National Host" (with ribbon)	2	$2500	$2700

1928, St. Moritz. "C.I.O.", $800-850.

1928, Amsterdam. "Officiel" (with rosette), $1100-1150.

1928, St. Moritz. "Officiel", $650-700.

1928, St. Moritz. "Presse", $650-700.

1932, Lake Placid. "Official", $2500-2800.

1932, Lake Placid. 'III OWG Committee" (with ribbon), $2500-2700.

1932, Los Angeles. "Press" (with ribbon), $550-600.

Year	City	Description	Rarity	Avg	Nr Mint
1932	Los Angeles	"Olympic Village" (with ribbon)	2	$700	$750
1932	Los Angeles	"Sports Technical" (with ribbon)	2	$700	$750
1932	Los Angeles	"X.O.C." (with ribbon)	2	$700	$750
1932	Los Angeles	"Xth Olympiad" (with ribbon)	2	$650	$700
1932	Los Angeles	"I.O.C." (with ribbon)	2	$800	$850
1932	Los Angeles	"Staff" (with ribbon)	3	$600	$650
1932	Los Angeles	"Official" (with ribbon)	3	$600	$650
1932	Los Angeles	"Press" (with ribbon)	3	$550	$600
1932	Los Angeles	Number on face (with ribbon)	3	$600	$650
1936	Berlin	Competitor's badge, numbered on face (with ribbon)	3	$550	$600
1936	Berlin	Worker's Badge (Bakelite)	3	$150	$175
1936	Berlin	"N.O.K." (with ribbon)	2	$1300	$1400
1936	Berlin	"Stab" (with ribbon)	3	$1700	$1800
1936	Berlin	"Presse" (with ribbon)	4	$400	$450

1932, Los Angeles. Number on face (with ribbon), $600-650.

1932, Los Angeles. "Sports Technical" (with ribbon), $700-750.

1936, Berlin. "N.O.K." (with ribbon), $1300-1400.

1936, Berlin. "Presse" (with ribbon), $400-450.

Year	City	Description	Rarity	Avg	Nr Mint
1936	Garmisch	"Presse" on reverse	3	$800	$900
1936	Garmisch	"Teilnehmer" on reverse	3	$700	$800
1936	Garmisch	"Presse" on reverse (with rosette)	2	$900	$1000
1940	Tokyo	"XII Olympiad Tokyo 1940" (committee, purple rosette)	1	$1500	$1600
1940	Tokyo	"XII Olympiad Tokyo 1940" (press, with green rosette)	1	$1500	$1600
1948	London	Competitor's bronze badge (with sport name on ribbon)	3	$220	$275
1948	London	Team Manager's bronze badge (with job title on ribbon)	3	$225	$275
1948	London	Official's silvered badge (with sport name on ribbon)	3	$350	$400
1948	St. Moritz	"Presse"	3	$450	$500
1948	St. Moritz	"Radio"	2	$1000	$1100
1948	St. Moritz	"Ski"	2	$1500	$1600
1948	St. Moritz	"Officiel"	3	$600	$650
1948	St. Moritz	"Concurrent"	3	$600	$650

1940, Tokyo. "XII Olympiad Tokyo 1940" (committee, purple rosette), $1500-1600.

1936, Garmisch. "Presse" on reverse (with rosette), $900-1000.

1936, Garmisch. "Teilnehmer" on reverse, $700-800.

1940, Tokyo. "XII Olympiad Tokyo 1940" (press, green rosette), $1500-1600.

1948, London. Competitor' s bronze badge (with sport name on ribbon), $220-275.

1948, London. Team Manager's bronze badge (with job title on ribbon), $225-275.

1948, London. Official's silvered badge (with sport name on ribbon), $350-400.

1948, St. Moritz. "Concurrent", $600-650.

Year	City	Description	Rarity	Avg	Nr Mint
1948	St. Moritz	"C.I.O."	2	$1000	$1100
1952	Helsinki	Athlete (with ribbon)	4	$250	$300
1952	Helsinki	Official (with ribbon)	3	$350	$400
1952	Helsinki	Radio (with ribbon)	3	$300	$400
1952	Helsinki	Jury (with ribbon)	3	$350	$400
1952	Helsinki	International Federation (with 2 ribbons)	3	$650	$700
1952	Helsinki	Press (with ribbon)	4	$250	$300
1952	Helsinki	Medical (with ribbon)	3	$600	$650
1952	Oslo	"Presse"	3	$500	$550
1952	Oslo	"Deltager" (athlete)	3	$500	$550
1952	Oslo	"Official"	3	$550	$600
1952	Oslo	"N.O.K."	3	$1500	$1600
1952	Oslo	"Radio"	2	$850	$900
1952	Oslo	"C.I.O."	2	$1500	$1600
1952	Oslo	Official guest badge	4	$300	$325

1948, St. Moritz. "Officiel", $600-650.

1948, St. Moritz. "Radio", $1000-1100.

1952, Helsinki. "C.O.N." (with 2 ribbons), $650-700.

1952, Helsinki. "FILM" media (with ribbon), $250-300.

1952, Oslo. "Deltager" (athlete), $500-550.

1952, Oslo. "Official", $550-600.

1952, Oslo. "Presse", $500-550.

Year	City	Description	Rarity	Avg	Nr Mint
1956	Cortina	Organizing Committee badge (small size)	3	$475	$525
1956	Cortina	"Atleta" (athlete)	3	$450	$500
1956	Cortina	"Stampa" (press)	3	$350	$375
1956	Cortina	Visitor's badge	4	$125	$150
1956	Cortina	"Presidente C.I.O." (with ribbon at top)	1	$2000	$2100
1956	Cortina	"C.N.O."	2	$1200	$1300
1956	Cortina	"Ufficiale"	3	$650	$700
1956	Cortina	Organizing Committee badge (large size)	3	$375	$400
1956	Cortina	"Aiutante"	3	$475	$500
1956	Melbourne	Official's badge (with ribbon)	3	$350	$400

1956, Cortina. "Stampa" (press), $350-375.

1956, Cortina. "Atleta" (athlete), $450-500.

1956, Cortina. "C.N.O.", $1200-1300.

1956, Melbourne. Athlete's badge (with ribbon), $350-400.

1956, Melbourne. Official's badge (with ribbon), $350-400.

Year	City	Description	Rarity	Avg	Nr Mint
1956	Melbourne	Press badge (with ribbon)	3	$350	$400
1956	Melbourne	Athlete's badge (with ribbon)	3	$350	$400
1956	Stockholm	Attache's badge (with 2 ribbons)	3	$650	$700
1956	Stockholm	Team captain's badge	3	$500	$550
1956	Stockholm	Organizing Committee badge (with 2 ribbons)	3	$400	$450
1956	Stockholm	Veterinarian's badge (purple)	3	$550	$575
1956	Stockholm	Official's badge (green)	3	$475	$500
1956	Stockholm	Team assistant badge	3	$450	$500
1960	Rome	"Servizio"	4	$300	$350
1960	Rome	"Capo Missione"	3	$400	$450
1960	Rome	"Servizio Sanitario"	3	$350	$400
1960	Rome	"Atleta"	4	$275	$300
1960	Rome	"Ufficiale"	4	$350	$400
1960	Rome	"Technico"	4	$300	$350
1960	Rome	"Comitato Organizzatore"	3	$400	$450
1960	Rome	"Radio-TV"	4	$300	$350
1960	Rome	"C.N.O."	3	$700	$750
1960	Rome	"Stampa"	4	$275	$300
1960	Rome	"Assistente"	4	$300	$350

1956, Stockholm. Official's badge (green), $475-500.

1956, Stockholm. Attache's badge (with 2 ribbons), $650-700.

1956, Stockholm. Organizing Committee badge (with 2 ribbons), $400-450.

Year	City	Description	Rarity	Avg	Nr Mint
1960	Squaw Valley	No badges issued			
1964	Innsbruck	"FIS"	3	$200	$225
1964	Innsbruck	"Presse"	4	$175	$200
1964	Innsbruck	"Wettkampfer" (athlete)	4	$225	$250
1964	Innsbruck	"Offiziell"	4	$150	$175
1964	Innsbruck	"NOC"	3	$250	$300
1964	Innsbruck	"OK" (Olympic Committee)	3	$400	$450
1964	Innsbruck	"Funktionar"	3	$150	$175
1964	Innsbruck	"Offizieller Fahrpark"	3	$200	$225
1964	Innsbruck	"Foto-Film"	3	$200	$225
1964	Innsbruck	"Bundespolizei"	3	$200	$225
1964	Innsbruck	"Bundesheer"	3	$150	$175
1964	Innsbruck	"Radio-TV"	4	$150	$175
1964	Tokyo	"XVIII Olympiad" (with ribbon)	3	$550	$600
1964	Tokyo	"Radio & TV" (with ribbon)	4	$400	$425
1964	Tokyo	"I.S.F. President" (with ribbon)	3	$800	$850
1964	Tokyo	"I.S.F. President" (with ribbon)	3	$1100	$1200
1964	Tokyo	"N.O.C." (with ribbon)	3	$800	$850
1964	Tokyo	"Chef De Mission" (with ribbon)	3	$900	$1000
1964	Tokyo	"Press" (with ribbon)	4	$500	$550
1964	Tokyo	"Competitor" (with ribbon)	4	$400	$425
1968	Grenoble	"C.O.J.O."	3	$325	$350
1968	Grenoble	"Invite"	3	$300	$325
1968	Grenoble	"C.N.O."	3	$550	$600
1968	Grenoble	"Officiel"	3	$300	$350
1968	Grenoble	"Delegation"	3	$250	$300
1968	Grenoble	Official Guest Badge	3	$275	$300
1968	Grenoble	"Presse"	4	$125	$150
1968	Grenoble	"C.N.O."	3	$325	$350
1968	Grenoble	"Concurrent"	4	$150	$175
1968	Grenoble	"C.I.O."	3	$500	$550
1968	Grenoble	"Chef De Mission"	3	$600	$625

1964, Innsbruck. "Presse", $175-200.

1964, Innsbruck. "Offiziell", $150-175.

1968, Grenoble. "C.N.O.", $550-600.

Year	City	Description	Rarity	Avg	Nr Mint
1968	Mexico City	"Juez" (judge, with plastic ribbon)	4	$275	$300
1968	Mexico City	"Technico" (with plastic ribbon)	4	$275	$300
1968	Mexico City	"Jefe De Mision"	3	$350	$375
1968	Mexico City	"Atleta" (athlete, with plastic ribbon)	4	$275	$300
1968	Mexico City	"Prensa" (press, with plastic ribbon)	4	$250	$275
1972	Munich	"Presse"	5	$100	$125
1972	Munich	"Mannschafts-offizieller"	4	4125	$150
1972	Munich	"Olympisches Jugendlager"	4	$125	$150
1972	Munich	"Jury"	4	$125	$150
1972	Munich	"Athlet"	5	$75	$100
1972	Munich	"Gast"	5	$100	$125

1968, Grenoble. "Chef De Mission", $600-625.

1968, Grenoble. "Concurrent", $150-175.

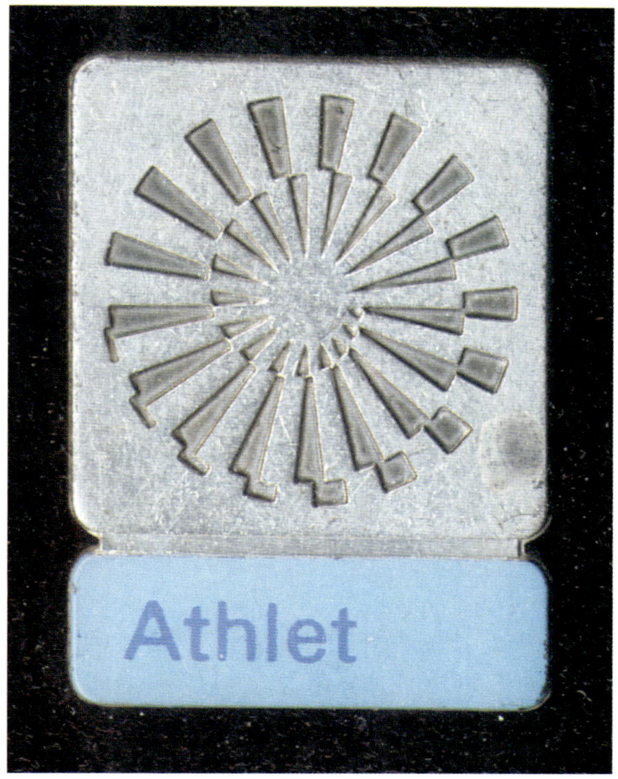

1972, Munich. "Athlet", $75-100.

1972, Munich. "Gast", $100-125.

Year	City	Description	Rarity	Avg	Nr Mint
1972	Munich	"Radio-TV"	4	$100	$125
1972	Munich	"Film"	4	$100	$125
1972	Munich	"NOK"	3	$125	$150
1972	Munich	"OBG"	4	$125	$150
1972	Munich	"Attache"	4	$100	$125
1972	Munich	"IF"	3	$250	$300
1972	Munich	"Kampfrichter"	4	$125	$150
1972	Munich	"IOC"	4	$150	$175
1972	Sapporo	"Photo" (with ribbon)	3	$700	$750
1972	Sapporo	"Committee" (with ribbon)	3	$600	$650
1972	Sapporo	"I.S.F. Jury" (with ribbon)	3	$600	$650
1972	Sapporo	"Team Official" (with ribbon)	3	$600	$650
1972	Sapporo	"Press" (with ribbon)	3	$550	$600
1972	Sapporo	"Radio & TV" (with ribbon)	3	$600	$650
1972	Sapporo	"Chef De Mission" (with ribbon)	3	$1000	$1100
1972	Sapporo	"Competitor" (with ribbon)	3	$550	$600
1972	Sapporo	"N.O.C." (with ribbon)	3	$450	$500
1976	Innsbruck	"Funktionar"	4	$125	$150
1976	Innsbruck	"Presse Radio-TV"	5	$100	$125
1976	Innsbruck	"Offiziell"	5	$100	$125
1976	Innsbruck	"Wettkampfer" (athlete)	5	$125	$150
1976	Innsbruck	Official Guest badge	4	$325	$350
1976	Innsbruck	"Bundesheer'	4	$125	$150
1976	Innsbruck	"O.K."	4	$150	$175
1976	Montreal	"Radio-TV"	5	$60	$75
1976	Montreal	"Medecin"	4	$250	$275
1976	Montreal	"Officiel Technique"	5	$125	$140
1976	Montreal	"CIO IOC"	4	$150	$175
1976	Montreal	"Concurrent"	5	$60	$80
1976	Montreal	"Officiel d'Equipe"	5	$75	$90
1976	Montreal	"Jury"	4	$100	$125
1976	Montreal	"Presse"	5	$60	$80
1976	Montreal	"FIS IFS"	4	$100	$125

1972, Munich. "Jury", $125-150.

1972, Sapporo. "I.S.F. Jury" (with ribbon), $600-650.

1972, Sapporo. "Press" (with ribbon), $550-600.

1976, Innsbruck. "Presse Radio-TV", $100-125.

PARTICIPATION MEDALS

Olympic Participation Medals have their origins with the first Modern Games held in Athens in 1896. Called officially "Commemoratives" these medals were presented to all athletes and officials as remembrances of the games. The medals are usually struck in bronze but there have been medals struck in steel, copper, pewter, and tombac (copper and zinc), and some have been plated in silver. The designs of the medals can be quite beautiful and are different in each Olympic Games. They can be produced in almost any size and made of any metal but official rules state they must be at least 3mm in thickness. Medallic art is a craft that can create beautiful objects. Participation medals have been round, oval, square, and rectangular. Depictions on the medals include athletes, animals, the Olympic flame, and the Olympic rings. Highly prized by collectors Participation Medals range from very common in availability to exceedingly rare.

GRADING PARTICIPATION MEDALS

Grading Olympic Participation Medals is very similar to coin grading. Condition is based on wear. However, medals tend to be valued more liberally when it comes to condition..

Average condition: Slight wear to high relief points. Possible tiny rim nicks. No major problems.

Near Mint condition: Out of the box quality. No visible naked eye flaws.

RARITY SCALE

See page 12.

Year	City	Description	Rarity	Avg	Nr Mint
1896	Athens	Bronze	3	$800	$1500
1900	Paris	None Issued			
1904	St. Louis	Copper	1	$13,000	$16,000
1906	Athens	Bronze	3	$400	$650
1908	London	Pewter	3	$275	$400
1912	Stockholm	Pewter	3	$250	$400
1920	Antwerp	Bronze	3	$250	$400

1896, Athens. Bronze participation medal, $800-1500.

1904, St. Louis. Participation medal, $13,000-16,000.

1912, Stockholm. Pewter participation medal, $250-400.

1906, Athens. Bronze participation medal, $400-650.

1920, Antwerp. Bronze participation medal, $250-400.

1908, London. Pewter participation medal, $275-400.

Year	City	Description	Rarity	Avg	Nr Mint
1924	Chamonix	Bronze	2	$7500	$8500
1924	Paris	Bronze	4	$250	$350
1928	St. Moritz	Bronze	3	$750	$1000
1928	Amsterdam	Bronze	4	$250	$350
1932	Lake Placid	Bronze	2	$3000	$4000
1932	Los Angeles	Bronze	3	$550	$750
1936	Garmish-Partenkirchen	Bronze	3	$900	$1200
1936	Berlin	Bronze	4	$250	$350

1924, Chamonix. Bronze participation medal, $7500-8500.

1924, Paris. Bronze participation medal, $250-350.

1928, St. Moritz. Bronze participation medal, $750-1000.

1928, Amsterdam. Bronze participation medal, $250-350.

1932, Lake Placid. Bronze participation medal, $3000-4000.

1932, Los Angeles. Bronze participation medal, $550-750.

1936, Garmish-Partenkirchen. Bronze participation medal, $900-1200.

1936, Berlin. Bronze participation medal, $250-350.

Year	City	Description	Rarity	Avg	Nr Mint
1948	St. Moritz	Bronze	3	$750	$1000
1948	London	Bronze	4	$225	$300
1952	Oslo	Copper	3	$800	$1150
1952	Helsinki	Bronze	5	$150	$225
1956	Cortina D'Ampezzo	Bronze	3	$600	$850
1956	Stockholm (Equestrian)	Bronze	2	$4000	$5500
1956	Melbourne	Bronze	4	$225	$325
1960	Squaw Valley	Bronze	3	$750	$1000

1952, Oslo. Copper participation medal, $800-1150.

1948, St. Moritz. Bronze participation medal, $750-1000.

1952, Helsinki. Bronze participation medal, $150-225.

1948, London. Bronze participation medal, $225-300.

1956, Cortina D'Ampezzo. Bronze participation medal, $600-850.

1956, Melbourne. Bronze participation medal, $225-325.

1956, Stockholm (Equestrian). Bronze participation medal, $4000-5500

1960, Squaw Valley. Bronze participation medal, $275-375.

Year	City	Description	Rarity	Avg	Nr Mint
1960	Rome	Bronze	5	$250	$350
1964	Innsbruck	Bronze	4	$250	$375
1964	Tokyo	Copper	4	$350	$450
1968	Grenoble	Bronze	4	$275	$375
1968	Mexico City	Copper	5	$125	$175
1972	Sapporo	Bronze	3	$600	$800
1972	Munich	Steel	4	$250	$325
1976	Innsbruck	Silvered Bronze	4	$275	$375

1964, Tokyo. Copper participation medal, $350-450.

1960, Rome. Bronze participation medal, $250-350.

1968, Grenoble. Bronze participation medal, $275-375.

1964, Innsbruck. Bronze participation medal, $250-375.

1972, Munich. Steel participation medal, $250-325.

1968, Mexico City. Copper participation medal, $125-175.

1976, Innsbruck. Silvered Bronze participation medal, $275-375.

1972, Sapporo. Bronze participation medal, $600-800.

Year	City	Description	Rarity	Avg	Nr Mint
1976	Montreal	Copper	5	$200	$275
1980	Lake Placid	Nickel Silver	4	$275	$350
1980	Moscow	Tombac	5	$150	$250
1984	Sarajevo	Bronze	3	$650	$725
1984	Los Angeles	Bronze	5	$175	$225
1988	Calgary	Bronze	3	$250	$325
1988	Seoul	Bronze	4	$200	$275
1992	Albertville	Chrome Plated Steel	3	$600	$800

1976, Montreal. Copper participation medal, $200-275.

1980, Lake Placid. Nickel Silver participation medal, $275-350.

1980, Moscow. Tomback participation medal, $150-250.

1984, Sarajevo. Bronze participation medal, $650-725.

1984, Los Angeles. Bronze participation medal, $175-225.

1988, Seoul. Bronze participation medal, $200-275.

1988, Calgary. Bronze participation medal, $250-325.

1992, Albertville. Chrome plated steel participation medal, $600-800.

Year	City	Description	Rarity	Avg	Nr Mint
1992	Barcelona	Burnished Copper	5	$125	$175
1994	Lillehammer	Copper	4	$200	$250
1996	Atlanta	Bronze	5	$100	$125
1998	Nagano	Bronze	4	$200	$250
2000	Sydney	Silver Plate	5	$100	$125

* Participation medals with original presentation boxes will add a premium to certain collectors. This is especially true with older medals.

1992, Barcelona. Burnished copper participation medal, $125-175.

1994, Lillehammer. Copper participation medal, $200-250.

1996, Atlanta. Bronze participation medal, $100-125.

1998, Nagano. Bronze participation medal, $200-250.

2000, Sydney. Silver plate participation medal, $100-150.

PRIZE MEDALS

The first Olympic prize medals (also called winner's medals or award medals) were awarded at the first modern Olympics held in Athens, Greece in 1896. Medals were presented to the first and second place finishers only. The first place finisher received a silver medal and the second place finisher a bronze medal. At the second Modern Games in 1900 the first gold medals were awarded, starting a tradition that continues to this day. However, in some events medals of different types were awarded to as many as 20 places. In 1904 only the first three finishers were recognized with medal awards. This became the standard followed today. Only four times have Olympic gold medals actually been made of solid gold (1900, 1904, 1908, and 1912). Since 1920, the "gold" medals were actually made of silver and plated in gold (known as gilding or vermeil). Prize medals are among the rarest Olympic collectibles. In 1896 only about 250 medals were awarded. Even today only about 2000 medals are awarded at a Summer Olympics, and less than 400 awarded at a Winter Olympics.

GRADING PRIZE MEDALS

Grading Prize Medals is similar to coin grading. Condition is based on wear. However, medals tend to be valued more liberally when it comes to condition.

Average Condition: Slight wear to high relief points. Possible tiny rim nicks. No major problems.

Near Mint Condition: Out of the box quality. No visible naked eye flaws.

RARITY SCALE

See page 12

Year	City	Description	Rarity	Avg	Nr Mint
1896	Athens	First Place/Silver	2	$8,000	$12,000

1896, Athens. First Place/Silver winner's medal, $8,000-12,000.

Year	City	Description	Rarity	Avg	Nr Mint
1896	Athens	Second Place/Bronze	2	$6,500	$10,000
1900	Paris	First Place (Golf) Gold	1	$6,000	$7,000
1900	Paris	[1]Gilt Silver	3	$1500	$2,000
1900	Paris	[1]Silver	4	$800	$1,200
1900	Paris	[1]Silvered Bronze	4	$600	$900
1900	Paris	[1]Bronze	4	$600	$900
1904	St. Louis	First Place/Gold	1	$10,000	$13,000
1904	St. Louis	Second Place/Silver	1	$9,000	$12,000
1904	St. Louis	Third Place/Bronze	1	$8,000	$10,000
1906	Athens	First Place/Gilt Silver	3	$4,000	$4,500
1906	Athens	Second Place/Silver	3	$3,000	$3,500
1906	Athens	Third Place/Bronze	3	$2,800	$3,200
1906	Athens	First Place Team/Silver with loop	2	$1,500	$2,000
1906	Athens	Second Place/Bronze with loop	2	$1,500	$2,000
1908	London	First Place/Gold	3	$3,800	$4,200
1908	London	Second Place/Silver	3	$3,500	$3,700
1908	London	Third Place/Bronze	3	$2,900	$3,200
1912	Stockholm	First Place/Gold	3	$3,200	$3,500
1912	Stockholm	First Place Team Winner/ Gilt Silver	3	$3,000	$3,400
1912	Stockholm	Second Place/Silver	3	$2,700	$2,900
1912	Stockholm	Third Place/Bronze	3	$2,000	$2,500
1920	Antwerp	First Place/Gilt Silver	4	$3,000	$3,700
1920	Antwerp	Second Place/Silver	4	$2,500	$2,900
1920	Antwerp	Third Place/Bronze	4	$1,500	$2,000
1924	Chamonix	First Place/Gilt Silver	2	$10,000	$12,000
1924	Chamonix	Second Place/Silver	2	$9,000	$11,000
1924	Chamonix	Third Place & Participant's Bronze	3	$7,500	$8,500
1924	Paris	First Place/Gilt Silver	3	$3,800	$4,400
1924	Paris	Second Place/Silver	3	$3,000	$3,700
1924	Paris	Third Place/Bronze	3	$2,800	$3,300
1928	St. Moritz	First Place/Gilt Silver	2	$5,000	$5,500
1928	St. Moritz	Second/Silver	2		
1928	St. Moritz	Third Place/Bronze	3	$3,200	$3,800
1928	Amsterdam	First Place/Gilt Silver	3	$4,000	$4,500
1928	Amsterdam	Second Place/Silver	3	$3,200	$4,000

1908, London. Second Place/Silver winner' s medal, $3,500-3,700.

1924, Chamonix. Third Place & participants Bronze winner's medal, $7,500-8,500.

1900, Paris. Silvered Bronze winner's medal, $600-900.

1928, St. Moritz. First Place/Gilt Silver winner's medal, $5,000-5,500.

Year	City	Description	Rarity	Avg	Nr Mint
1928	Amsterdam	Third Place/Bronze	3	$3,000	$3,500
1932	Lake Placid	First Place/Gilt Silver	1	$12,000	$15,000
1932	Lake Placid	Second Place/Silver	1	$11,500	$13,500
1932	Lake Placid	Third Place/Bronze	1	$11,000	$13,000
1932	Los Angeles	First Place/Gilt Silver	3	$4,000	$5,000
1932	Los Angeles	Second Place/Silver	3	$3,500	$4,000
1932	Los Angeles	Third Place/Bronze	3	$2,800	$3,300
1936	Garmisch-Partenkirchen	First Place/Gilt Silver	1	$15,000	$20,000
1936	Garmisch-Partenkirchen	Second Place/Silver	1	$13,000	$19,000
1936	Garmisch-Partenkirchen	Third Place/Bronze	1	$12,000	$18,000
1936	Berlin	First Place/Gilt Silver	3	$4,000	$5,000
1936	Berlin	Second Place/Silver	3	$3,500	$4,000
1936	Berlin	Third Place/Bronze	3	$3,000	$3,500
1948	St. Moritz	First Place/Gilt Silver	2	$5,000	$6,000
1948	St. Moritz	Second Place/Silver	2	$4,500	$5,500
1948	St. Moritz	Third Place/Bronze	2	$4,000	$5,000

1928, Amsterdam. First Place/Gilt Silver winner's medal, $4,000-4,500.

1936, Garmisch-Partenkirchen. Third Place/Bronze winner's medal, $12,000-18,000.

1932, Lake Placid. Third Place/Bronze winner's medal, $11,000-15,000.

1948, St. Moritz. Third Place/Bronze winner's medal, $4,000-5,000.

Year	City	Description	Rarity	Avg	Nr Mint
1948	London	First Place/Gilt Silver	3	$4,000	$4,500
1948	London	Second Place/Silver	3	$3,500	$4,000
1948	London	Third Place/Bronze	3	$3,000	$3,500
1952	Oslo	First Place/Gilt Silver	2	$6,000	$7,000
1952	Oslo	Second Place/Silver	2	$5,500	$6,500
1952	Oslo	Third Place/Bronze	2	$5,000	$5,500
1952	Helsinki	First Place/Gilt Silver	3	$9,500	$4,200
1952	Helsinki	Second Place/Silver	3	$3,000	$3,500
1952	Helsinki	Third Place/Bronze	3	$2,800	$3,000
1956	Cortina D'Ampezzo	First Place/Gilt Silver	4	$3,500	$4,000
1956	Cortina D'Ampezzo	Second Place/Silver	4	$3,000	$3,500
1956	Cortina D'Ampezzo	Third Place/Bronze	4	$2,000	$2,500
1956	Stockholm (Equestrian)	First Place/Gilt Silver	1	$7,000	$8,000
1956	Stockholm (Equestrian)	Second Place/Silver	1	$6,500	$7,000
1956	Stockholm (Equestrian)	Third Place/Bronze	1	$6,000	$6,500
1956	Melbourne	First Place/Gilt Silver	4	$3,500	$4,000
1956	Melbourne	Second Place/Silver	4	$3,000	$3,500
1956	Melbourne	Third Place/Bronze	4	$2,500	$3,000
1960	Squaw Valley	First Place/Gilt Silver	2	$5,500	$6,000
1960	Squaw Valley	Second Place/Silver	2	$4,500	$5,500
1960	Squaw Valley	Third Place/Bronze	3	$3,500	$4,500
1960	Rome	First Place/Gilt Silver	3	$4,500	$5,500
1960	Rome	Second Place/Silver	3	$4,000	$4,500
1960	Rome	Third Place/Bronze	3	$3,000	$3,500
1964	Innsbruck	First Place/Gilt Silver	3	$5,000	$6,000
1964	Innsbruck	Second Place/Silver	3	$4,500	$5,500
1964	Innsbruck	Third Place/Bronze	3	$4,000	$5,000
1964	Tokyo	First Place/Gilt Silver	3	$5,000	$5,500
1964	Tokyo	Second Place/Silver	3	$4,500	$5,000
1964	Tokyo	Third Place/Bronze	3	$3,500	$4,000
1968	Grenoble	First Place/Gilt Silver	2	$5,500	$6,000
1968	Grenoble	Second Place/Silver	2	$4,500	$5,000
1968	Grenoble	Third Place/Bronze	2	$3,500	$4,000
1968	Mexico City	First Place/Gilt Silver	4	$4,500	$5,000
1968	Mexico City	Second Place/Silver	4	$3,500	$4,000
1968	Mexico City	Third Place/Bronze	4	$3,000	$3,500
1972	Sapporo	First Place/Gilt Silver	2	$6,000	$6,500
1972	Sapporo	Second Place/Silver	2	$5,500	$6,000
1972	Sapporo	Third Place/Bronze	2	$4,500	$5,500
1972	Munich	First Place/Gilt Silver	4	$4,500	$5,000
1972	Munich	Second Place/Silver	4	$3,500	$4,500
1972	Munich	Third Place/Bronze	4	$3,000	$3,500
1976	Innsbruck	First Place/Gilt Silver	2	$5,000	$6,000
1976	Innsbruck	Second Place/Silver	2	$4,500	$5,500
1976	Innsbruck	Third Place/Bronze	2	$4,000	$5,000
1976	Montreal	First Place/Gilt Silver	4	$4,000	$5,000
1976	Montreal	Second Place/Silver	4	$3,000	$4,000
1976	Montreal	Third Place/Bronze	4	$2,500	$3,500
1980	Lake Place	First Place/Gilt Silver	2	$6,000	$7,000
1980	Lake Placid	Second Place/Silver	2	$5,000	$6,000
1980	Lake Placid	Third Place/Bronze	2	$4,000	$5,000

1956, Cortina D'Ampezzo. Second Place/Silver winner's medal, $3,000-3,500.

1956, Stockholm (Equestrian). Second Place/Silver winner's medal, $6,500-7,000.

1956, Melbourne. Third Place/Bronze winner's medal, $2,500-3,000.

1964, Tokyo. Second Place/Silver winner's medal, $4,500-5,000.

1972, Sapporo. Second Place/Silver winner's medal, $5,500-6,000.

1972, Munich. Second Place/Silver winner's medal, $3,500-4,500.

1980, Lake Placid. Second Place/Silver winner's medal, $5,000-6,000.

Year	City	Description	Rarity	Avg	Nr Mint
1980	Moscow	First Place/Gilt Silver	4	$4,000	$4,500
1980	Moscow	Second Place/Silver	4	$3,000	$4,000
1980	Moscow	Third Place/Tombac	4	$2,500	$3,500
1984	Sarajevo	First Place/Gilt Silver	2	$6,000	$7,000
1984	Sarajevo	Second Place/Silver	2	$5,000	$6,000
1984	Sarajevo	Third Place/Bronze	2	$4,000	$3,500
1984	Los Angeles	First Place/Gilt Silver	3	$4,500	$6,000
1984	Los Angeles	Second Place/Silver	3	$4,000	$5,000
1984	Los Angeles	Third Place/Bronze	3	$3,000	$4,000
1988	Calgary	First Place/Gilt Silver	2	$5,500	$6,500
1988	Calgary	Second Place/Silver	2	$5,000	$6,000
1988	Calgary	Third Place/Bronze	2	$4,000	$5,000
1988	Seoul	First Place/Gilt Silver	4	$4,000	$5,000
1988	Seoul	Second Place Silver	4	$3,000	$4,000
1988	Seoul	Third Place/Bronze	4	$2,500	$3,500
1992	Albertville	First Place/Gilt Silver	2	$6,000	$7,000
1992	Albertville	Second Place/Silver	2	$5,500	$6,500
1992	Albertville	Third Place/Bronze	2	$5,000	$5,500
1992	Barcelona	First Place/Gilt Silver	4	$4,000	$5,000

1984, Sarajevo. First Place/Gilt Silver winner's medal, $6,000-7,000.

1996, Atlanta. First Place/Gilt Silver winner's medal, $5,500-6,500.

Year	City	Description	Rarity	Avg	Nr Mint
1992	Barcelona	Second Place/Silver	4	$3,000	$4,000
1992	Barcelona	Third Place/Bronze	4	$2,000	$3,000
1994	Lillehammer	First Place/Gilt Silver	2	$6,500	$7,000
1994	Lillehammer	Second Place/Silver	2	$6,000	$6,500
1994	Lillehammer	Third Place/Bronze	2	$5,000	$5,500
1996	Atlanta	First Place/Gilt Silver	3	$5,500	$6,500
1996	Atlanta	Second Place/Silver	3	$4,500	$5,500
1996	Atlanta	Third Place/Bronze	3	$3,500	$4,000
1998	Nagano	First Place/Gilt Silver	3	$7,000	$8,000
1998	Nagano	Second Place/Silver	2	$7,000	$8,000
1998	Nagano	Third Place/Bronze	2	$5,500	$6,500
2000	Sydney	First Place/Gilt Silver	3	$5,000	$5,500
2000	Sydney	Second Place/Silver	3	$4,000	$4,500
2000	Sydney	Third Place/Bronze	3	$3,000	$3,500

[1]Each sport had different methods of awarding medals. Medals were awarded for 2nd to, in some instances, 20th place. First place winners were awarded artwork or other prizes.

*Prize medals with original presentation boxes will add a premium to certain collectors. This is especially true with older medals.

2000, Sydney. Second Place/Silver winner's medal, $4,000-4,500.

1998, Nagano. Second Place/Silver winner's medal, $7,000-8,000.

OLYMPIC TORCHES

One of the most dramatic events of an Olympic Games is the Olympic Torch Relay. No other aspect of an Olympic Games is seen in person by as many people. The relay involves thousands of people and covers much of a host country's geography. It is one of the few chances for the average person to have a sense of involvement with the Olympic Games.

The Olympic Torch itself is based on ancient Greek artwork. Pictures of runners carrying a flame are a common theme. The first Olympic Games to have an Olympic Torch relay was the 1936 Summer Olympic held in Berlin, Germany. The flame was ignited by the sun in Olympia, Greece, site of the ancient Olympics, and carried by a relay of runners and torches to Berlin. The torch then ignited a huge caldron at the Olympic Stadium. The relay proved to be such a success, that it became an important part of the Olympic Games. The first Winter Olympic Torch Relay was held during the Oslo Games of 1952.

The quantity of torches produced for a particular Olympic varies greatly. For some Games only 10 or so torches are made, while for others 10,000 or more are produced.

1936, Berlin. Steel torch, $2000-3000.

GRADING OLYMPIC TORCHES

Olympic torches are graded based on the condition of the finish, and the amount of scratches and dents. Some torches are finished in natural metal coloring while others are enameled and plated.

Average Condition: Torch may have a small amount of scuffing, perhaps a small dent or two, and possibly a scratch or two.

Near Mint: Torch would have no blemishes, no scratches, and an almost perfect finish. If a torch shows signs of burn marks from the flame, it does not necessarily affect the value up or down.

RARITY SCALE

See page 12

Year	City	Description	Rarity	Avg	Nr Mint
1936	Berlin	27cm, steel	4	$2000	$3000
1948	London	47cm, White metal	3	$3500	$4500
1948	St. Moritz	No Torch			
1952	Oslo	Chromed metal with brass burner	1	$25,000	$35,000
1952	Helsinki	Silvered bowl with wood handle	1	$25,000	$35,000

1948, London. White metal torch, $3,500-4,500.

Year	City	Description	Rarity	Avg	Nr Mint
1956	Cortina D'Ampezzo	White metal	2	$6,000	$7,000
1956	Melbourne	47cm, White metal	3	$5,500	$7,000
1960	Squaw Valley	52cm, Aluminum alloy	1	$20,000	$35,000
1960	Rome	39.5cm, Bronzed aluminum	3	$4,000	$5,500

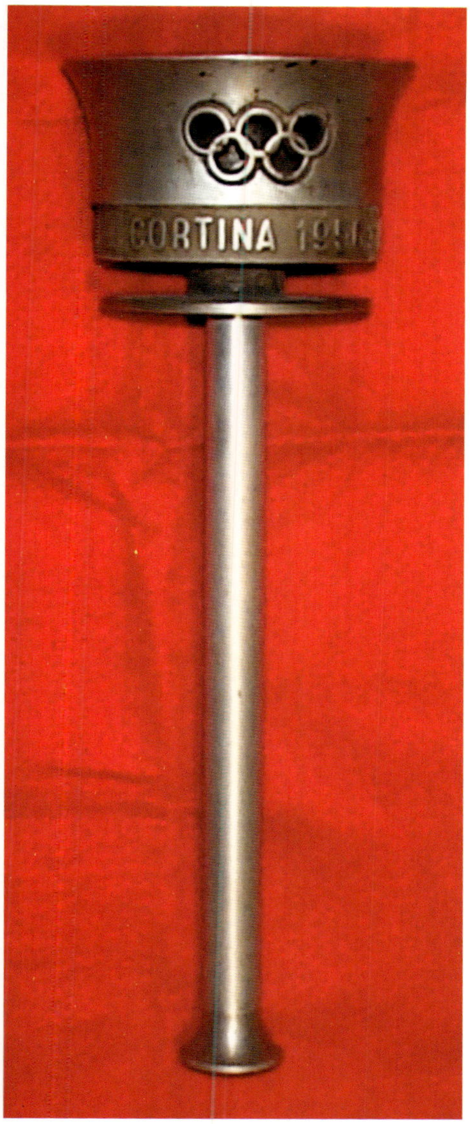

1956, Cortina D'Ampezzo. White metal torch, $6,000-7,000.

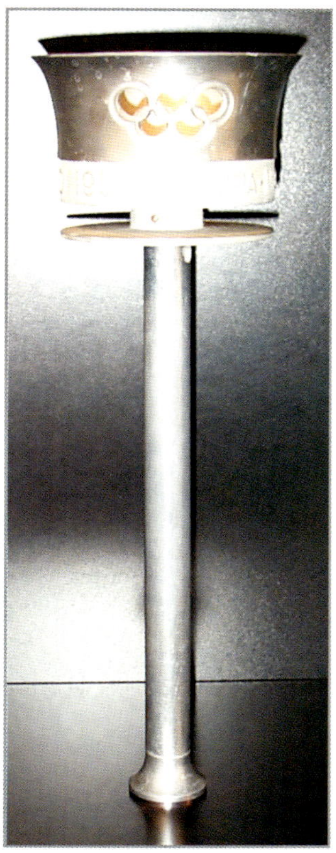

1956, Melbourne. White metal torch, $5,500-7,000.

1960, Squaw Valley. Aluminum alloy torch, $20,000-35,000.

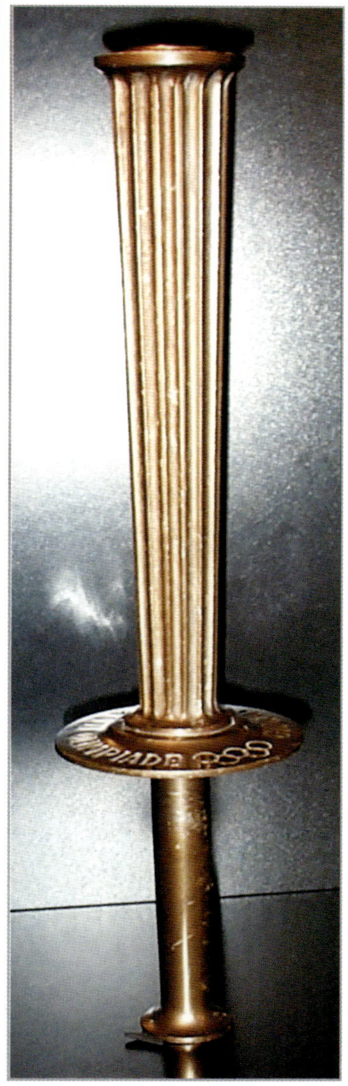

1960, Rome. Bronzed aluminum torch, $4,000-5,500.

Year	City	Description	Rarity	Avg	Nr Mint
1964	Innsbruck	Bronzed with steel burner	1	$10,000	$20,000
1964	Tokyo	65cm, Blackened aluminum alloy bowl/cylinder stainless steel clad	3	$4500	$5500
1968	Grenoble	Bronzed with material covered handle	1	$12,000	$16,000
1968	Mexico City	Silver-colored tin and partial wood shaft	4	$1,200	$2,000
1968	Mexico City	45cm, Cast white metal	4	$2,000	$2,200
1968	Mexico City	45cm, Cast white metal with black leather handle	4	$1,200	$2,000
1968	Mexico City	52cm, black, painted sheet metal with partial wood handle	4	$1,200	$2,400
1968	Mexico City	53cm, Silvered sheet metal with partial wood handle	4	$1,200	$2,000
1972	Munich	73cm, steel	5	$1,200	$2,000

1972, Munich. Steel torch, $1,200-2,000.

1964, Tokyo. Blackened aluminum alloy bowl/cylinder stainless steel clad torch, $4,500-5,500.

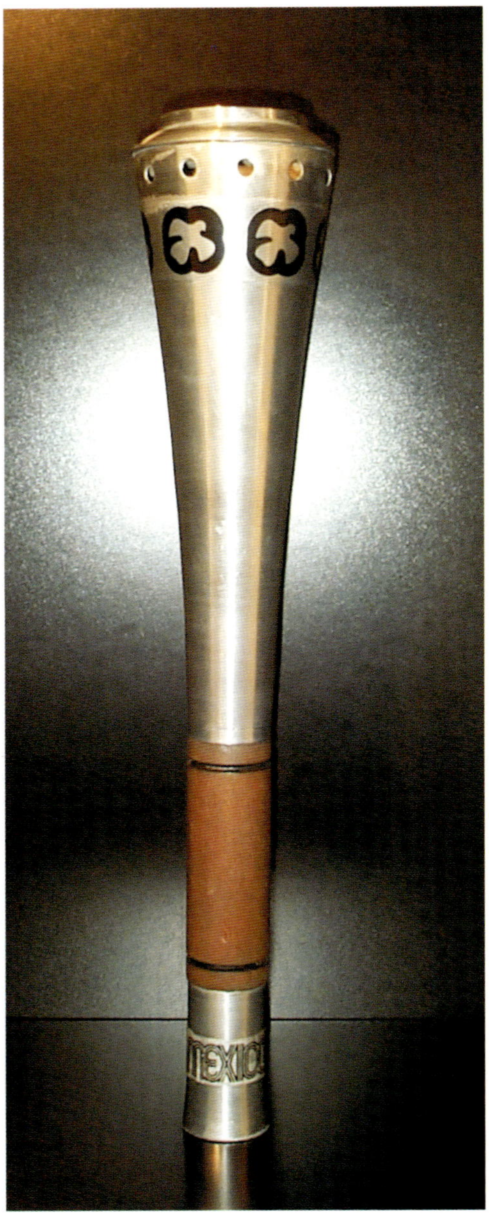

1968, Mexico City. Sheet metal with partial wood handle torch, $1,200-2,400.

Year	City	Description	Rarity	Avg	Nr Mint
1972	Sapporo	65cm, Blackened aluminum alloy bowl/cylinder stainless steel clad	2	$6,000	$8,000
1976	Montreal	66cm, Aluminum stem red, top black	4	$1,800	$2,800
1976	Innsbruck	74.5cm, aluminum	3	$5,000	$9,000

1976, Montreal. Aluminum stem red top black torch, $1,800-2,800.

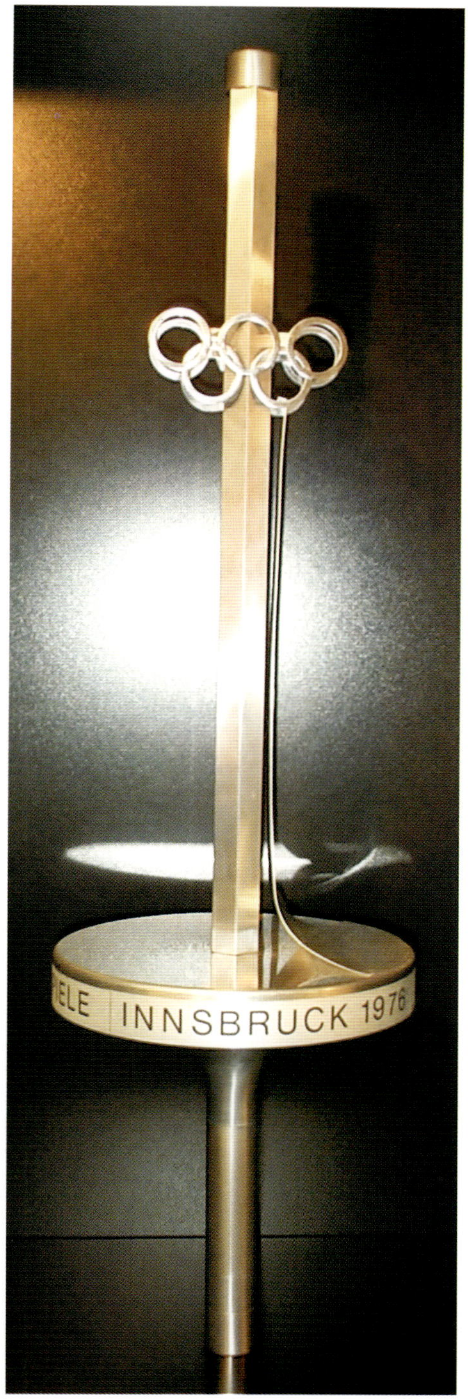

1976, Innsbruck. Aluminum torch, $5,000-9,000.

1972, Sapporo. Blackened aluminum alloy bowl/cylinder stainless steel clad torch, $6,000-8,000.

Year	City	Description	Rarity	Avg	Nr Mint
1980	Lake Placid	71cm, Bronzed bowl with tan leather handle	2	$8,000	$10,000
1980	Moscow	56cm, aluminum alloy grey and gold colored	5	$800	$1,500
1984	Sarajevo	57.5cm, stainless steel cylinder aluminum alloy bowl	3	$6,000	$7,000
1984	Los Angeles	56cm, Brass finished aluminum with tan leather handle	5	$1,200	$2,000

1984, Los Angeles. Brass finished aluminum with tan leather handle torch, $1,200-2,000.

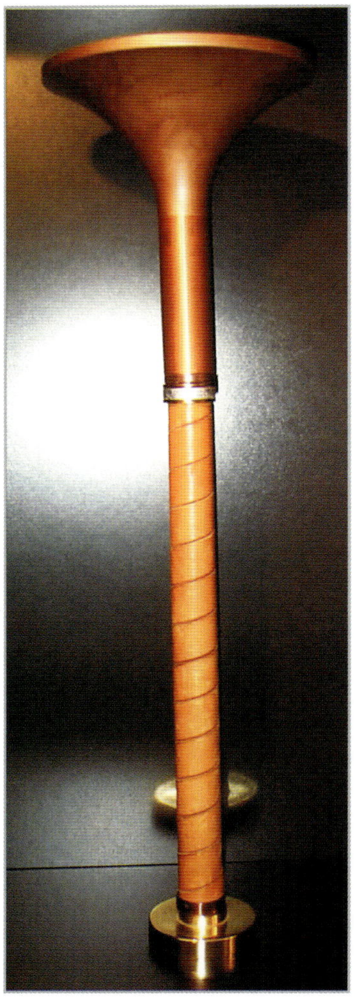

1980, Lake Placid. Bronzed bowl with tan leather handle torch, $8,000-10,000.

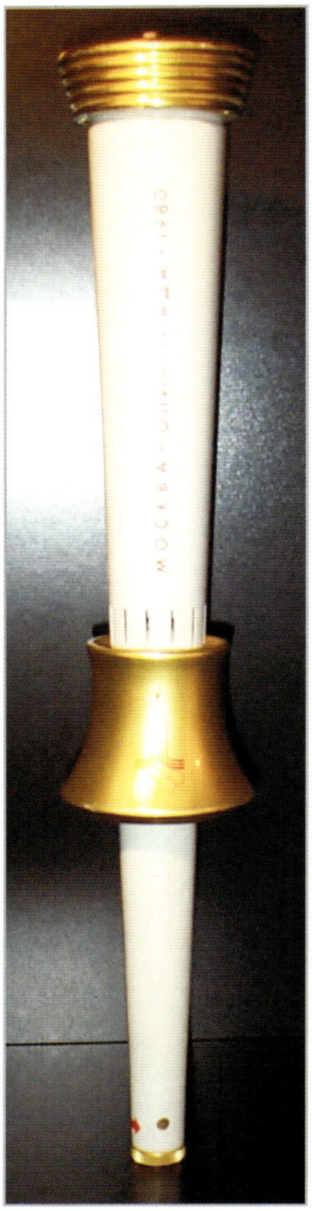

1980, Moscow. Aluminum alloy grey and gold colored torch, $800-1,500.

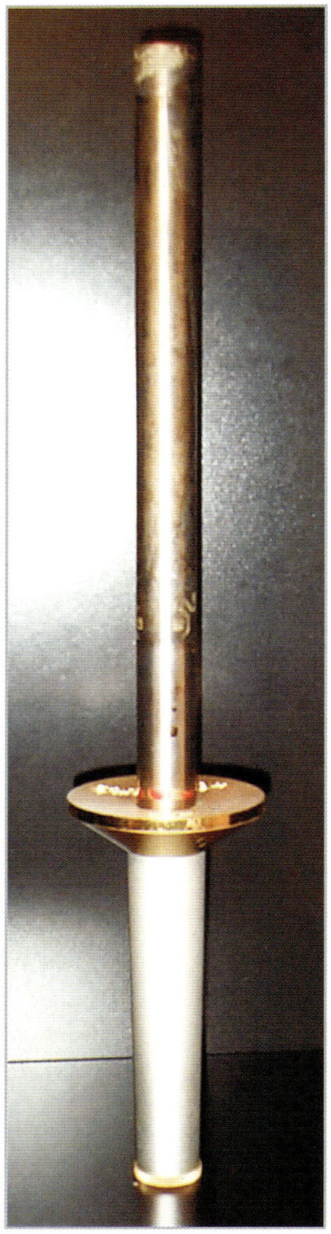

1984, Sarajevo. Stainless steel cylinder aluminum alloy bowl torch, $6,000-7,000.

Year	City	Description	Rarity	Avg	Nr Mint
1988	Calgary	58.5cm, Wood engraved handle with silvered bowl and handle knob	2	$8,000	$9,000
1988	Seoul	3 Sizes produced, brass, with tan leather handle	4	$2,000	$2,800
1992	Albertville	Horn-shaped, anodized metal	1	$8,000	$12,000
1992	Barcelona	65cm, chrome plated aluminum	4	$2,900	$3,500

1992, Barcelona. Chrome plated aluminum torch, $2,900-3,500.

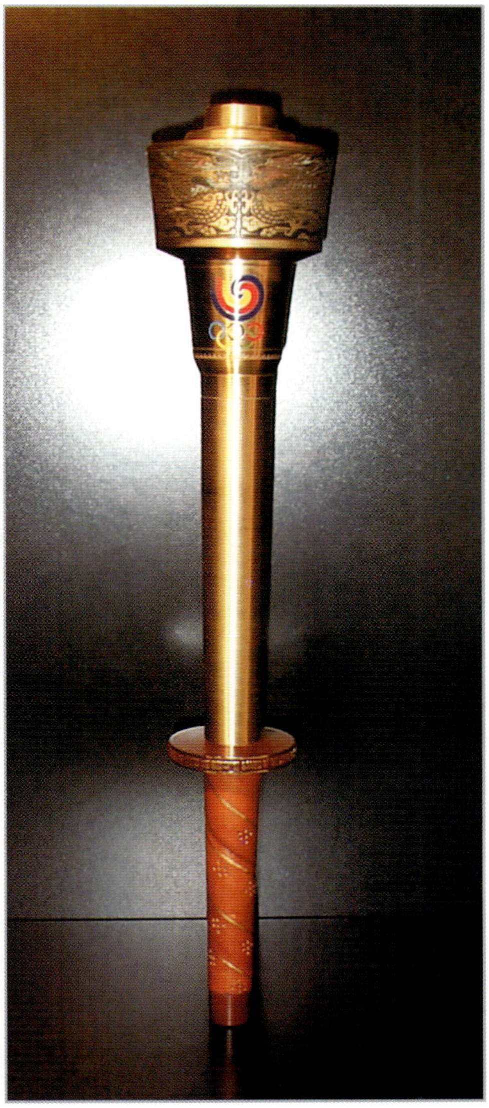

1988, Seoul. Brass with tan leather handle torch, $2,000-2,800.

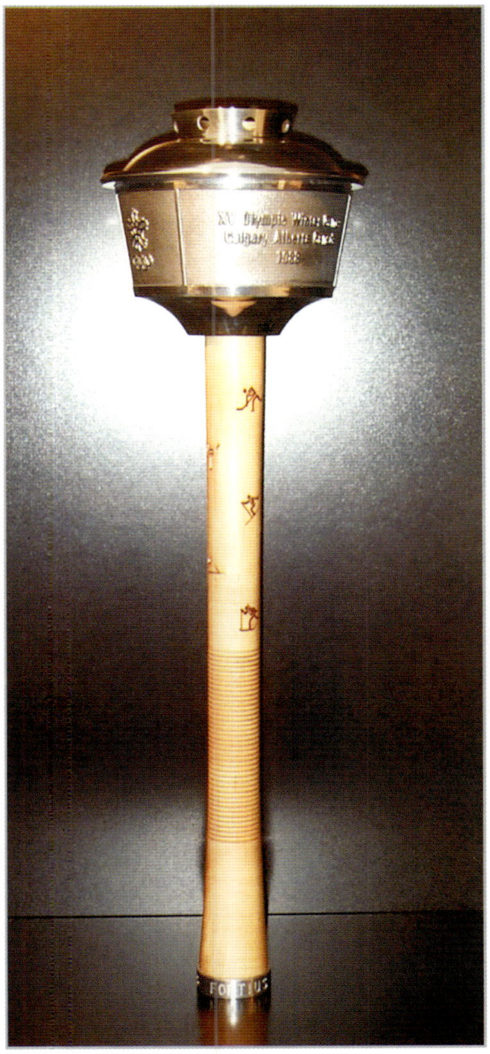

1988, Calgary. Wood engraved handle with silvered bowl and handle knob torch, $8,000-9,000.

Year	City	Description	Rarity	Avg	Nr Mint
1994	Lillehammer	147cm, Horn-shaped silvered and bronzed sheet metal top with wood handle	3	$5,500	$6,500
1996	Atlanta	80cm, Aluminum and Georgia pecan wood	5	$1,000	$1,500
1998	Nagano	55cm, Partially gilded aluminum with cord wrapped handle cord	3	$7,000	$8,000
2000	Sydney	77cm, 3 layers of different metals	4	$1,800	$2,000

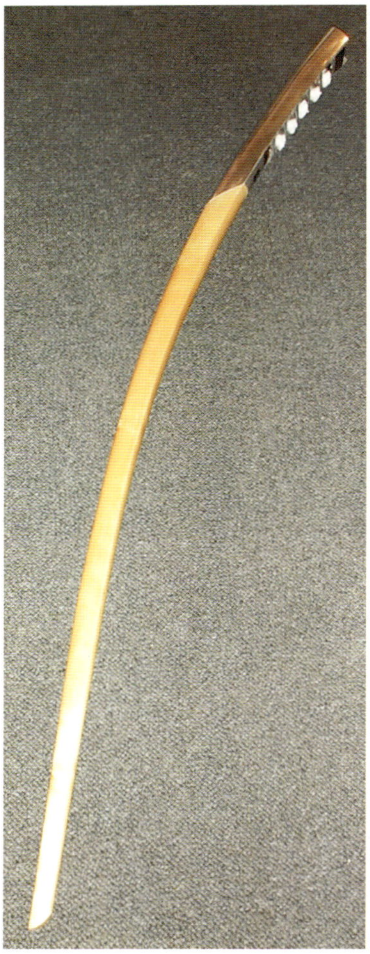

1994, Lillehammer. Horn shaped silvered and bronzed sheet metal top with wood handle torch, $5,500-6,500.

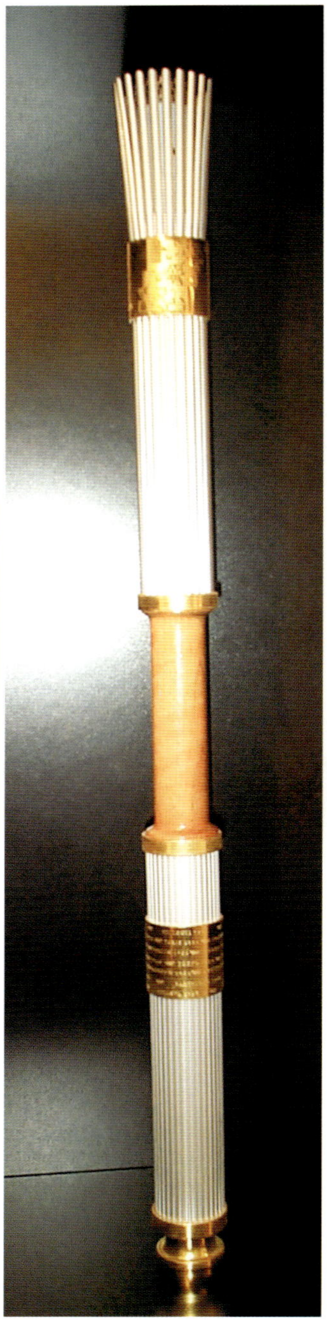

1996, Atlanta. Aluminum and Georgia pecan wood torch, $1,000-1,500.

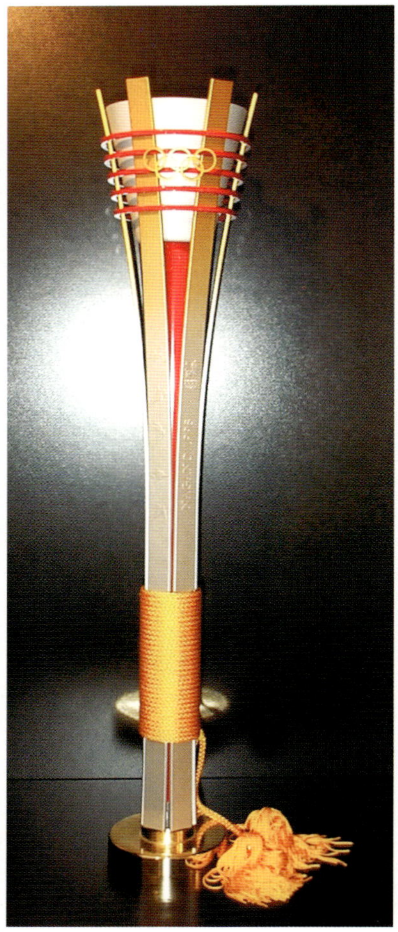

1998, Nagano. Partially gilded aluminum with corn wrapped handle cord torch, $7,000-8,000.

2000, Sydney. 3 Layers of different metals torch, $1,800-2,000.

OLYMPIC TICKETS

Olympic tickets have taken on many forms throughout the years. The first Olympic tickets in 1896 were printed on plain paper. In other years Olympic tickets have been printed on cardboard, cellulose, or even silk! Olympic tickets are among the most attractive admission tickets produced. Many have great graphics, bold colors, or are printed in large sizes making them very collectible. Olympic tickets include daily admission, season passes, and official tickets for media and V.I.P.s. One of the nice things about Olympic tickets is that you can acquire many of the earlier tickets for well under $50 each. However, some Olympic tickets command premiums because they were for specific events of significance. For example a ticket from the 1980 Lake Placid Winter Olympic USA vs. USSR hockey game carries a significant value increase over a regular hockey ticket from that Olympic Games.

GRADING OLYMPIC TICKETS

Olympic tickets are graded on quality of printing and lose value if there are any imperfections such as creases, folds, tears, or stains, etc. Also of importance is whether the ticket is unused (full), or used (stub).

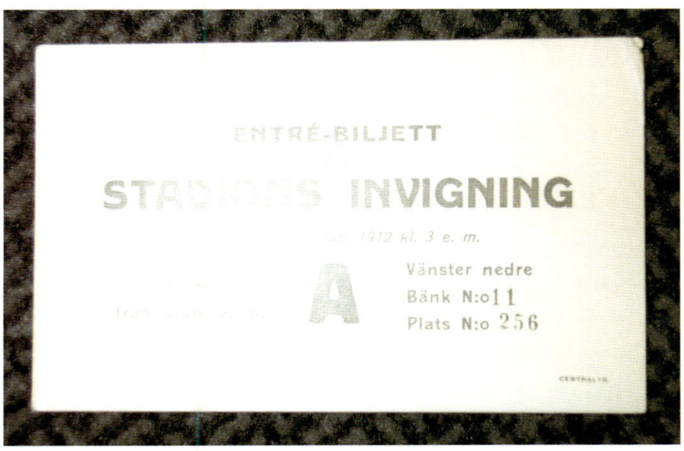

1912, Stockholm. Event admission ticket, $200-300.

Average condition: May have a slight crease or soft corner but no tears or stains. May be a ticket stub or full ticket.

Near Mint: No creasing, tears or staining. Possible soft corner, ink rub or other very minor problem. A near mint ticket must be an unused full ticket, not a stub.

RARITY SCALE

See page 12.

Year	City	Description	Rarity	Avg	Nr Mint
1896	Athens	[1]Single admission	1	$2500	$2500
1900	Paris	Exposition admission	4	$50	$75
1904	St. Louis	Exposition admission	4	$50	$200
1906	Athens	[1]Single admission	1	$400	$500
1908	London	Single admission	3	250	$300
1912	Stockholm	Event admission	3	$200	$300

1904, St. Louis. Exposition admission ticket, $50-200.

Year	City	Description	Rarity	Avg	Nr Mint
1912	Stockholm	Season Pass	3	$200	$300
1920	Antwerp	[1]Single admission	2	$400	$400
1924	Chamonix	[1]Single admission	1	$1000	$1000
1924	Paris	Single admission	3	250	400
1928	St. Moritz	[1]Single admission	1	$850	$800
1928	Amsterdam	Event admission	3	$120	$175
1928	Amsterdam	Season Pass	3	$120	$175
1932	Lake Placid	Single admission paper	4	$65	$100

1932, Los Angeles. Multiple ticket season pass ticket, $125-175.

1932, Lake Placid. Single admission paper ticket, $65-100.

1936, Garmisch-Partenkirchen. Single admission paper ticket, $175-225.

1932, Lake Placid. Single admission Celluloid paper ticket, $55-75.

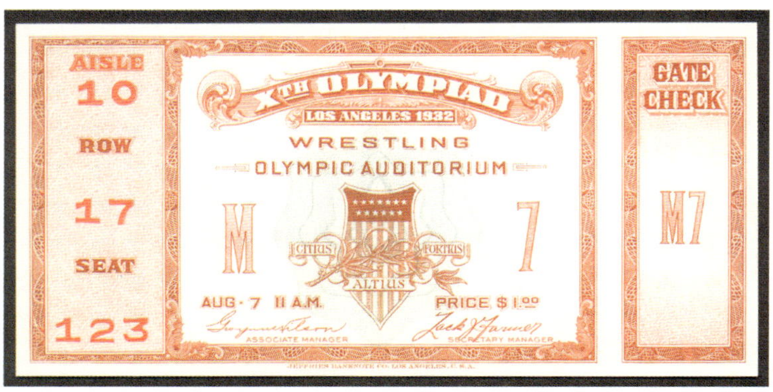

1932, Los Angeles. Single admission multiple ticket season pass ticket, $125-175.

1936. Garmisch-Partenkirchen. Silk ticket, $200-250.

Year	City	Description	Rarity	Avg	Nr Mint
1932	Lake Placid	Single admission Celluloid 3 colors produced	4	$55	$75
1932	Los Angeles	Single admission multiple ticket season pass	3	$125	$175
1932	Los Angeles	Multiple ticket season pass	3	$125	$175
1936	Garmisch-Partenkirchen	Single admission paper	2	$175	$225
1936	Garmisch-Partenkirchen	Silk ticket (Alpine skiing, bobsled)	2	$200	$250
1936	Berlin	Single admission	4	$50	$100
1948	St. Moritz	*Single admission	1	$300	$500
1948	London	Single admission	5	$35	$50
1952	Oslo	Single admission	4	$60	$75

1936, Berlin. Single admission ticket, $50-100.

1936. Garmisch-Partenkirchen. Silk ticket, $200-250.

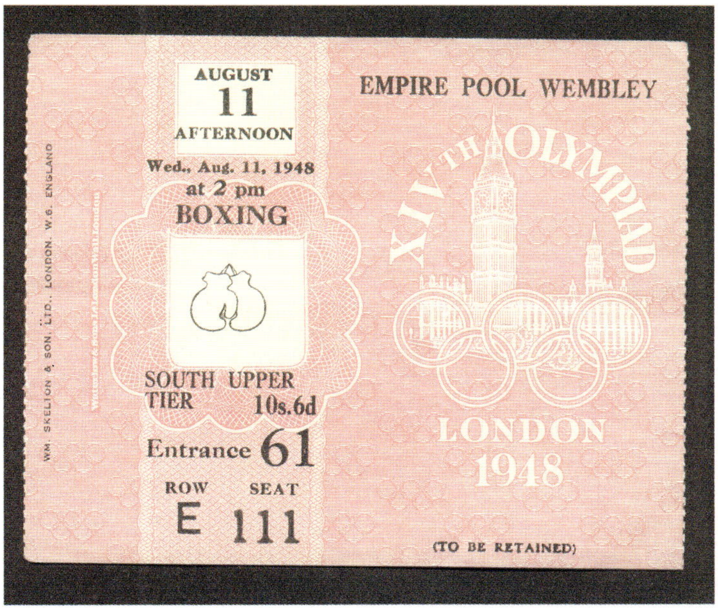

1948, London. Single admission ticket, $35-50.

1952, Oslo. Single admission ticket, $50-75.

Year	City	Description	Rarity	Avg	Nr Mint
1952	Helsinki	Single admission	5	$25	$30
1956	Cortina d'Ampezzo	Single admission	3	$150	$200
1956	Stockholm	Equestrian single admission	3	$150	$175
1956	Melbourne	Single admission	5	$20	$25
1960	Squaw Valley	Valley Daily	4	$75	$95
1960	Squaw Valley	Reserved seats	3	$175	$250
1960	Rome	Single admission	5	$25	$40

1952, Helsinki. Single admission ticket, $25-30.

1960, Squaw Valley. Daily ticket, $75-95.

1956, Cortina D'Ampezzo. Single admission ticket, $150-200.

1960, Rome. Single admission ticket, $25-40.

Year	City	Description	Rarity	Avg	Nr Mint
1964	Innsbruck	Single admission	4	$50	$75
1964	Tokyo	Single admission	4	$65	$85
1968	Grenoble	Single admission	4	$90	$125
1968	Mexico City	Single admission	5	$30	$40

1964, Innsbruck. Single admission ticket, $50-75.

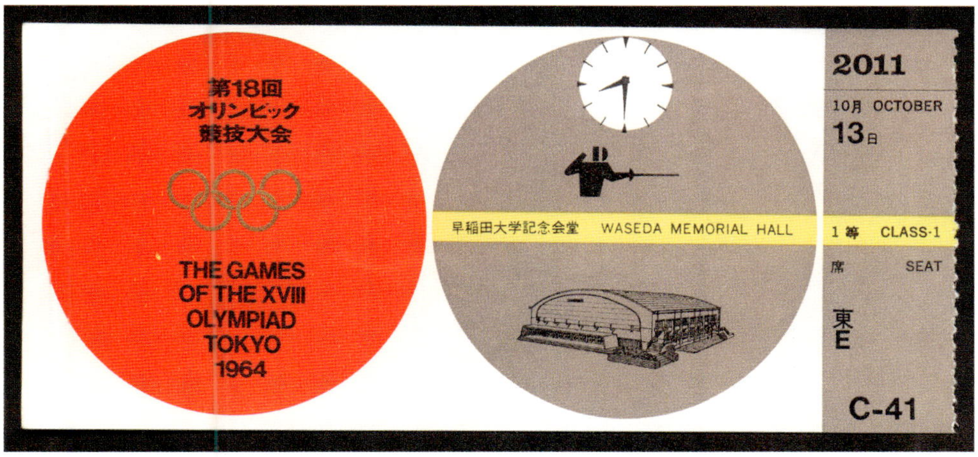

1964, Tokyo. Single admission ticket, $54-85.

1968, Grenoble. Single admission ticket, $90-125.

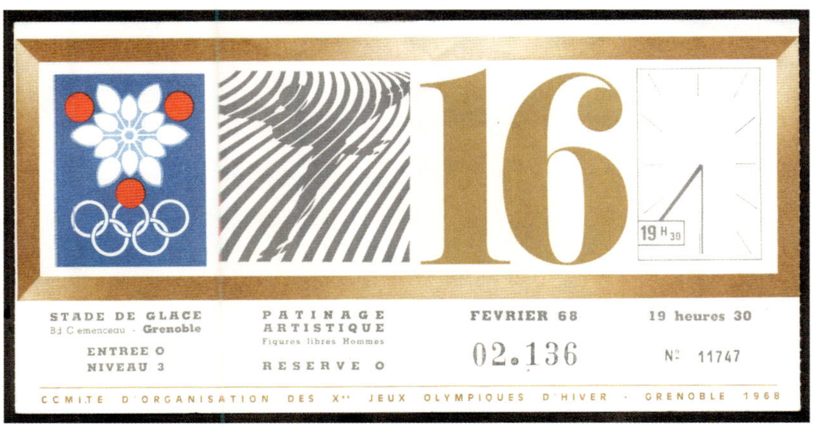

1968. Grenoble. Single admission ticket, $90-125.

1968, Mexico City. Single admission ticket, $30-40.

Year	City	Description	Rarity	Avg	Nr Mint
1972	Sapporo	Single admission	4	$65	$75
1972	Munich	Single admission	5	$20	$25
1976	Montreal	Multicolored paper ticket	4	$15	$20
1976	Innsbruck	Light card stock with pictogram of sport	3	440	$50
1980	Lake Placid	General admission	5	$10	$20
1980	Lake Placid	[2]Hockey U.S. vs. Russia "Miracle on Ice"	4	$300	$450
1980	Lake Placid	[3]Hockey U.S. vs. Finland "Final Round Game	4	$100	$150
1980	Moscow	Single admission	5	$20	$25
1984	Sarajevo	Single admission	4	$30	$40
1984	Los Angeles	Single admission	5	$10	$15
1988	Calgary	Single admission	5	$15	$20
1988	Seoul	Single admission	4	$20	$25
1992	Albertville	Single admission	5	$10	$15
1992	Barcelona	Single admission	5	$15	$20

1976, Montreal. Multicolored paper ticket, $15-20.

1976, Innsbruck. Light card stock with pictogram of sport ticket, $40-50.

1972, Sapporo. Single admission ticket, $65-75.

1980, Lake Placid. General admission ticket, $20-25.

1972, Munich. Single admission ticket, $20-25.

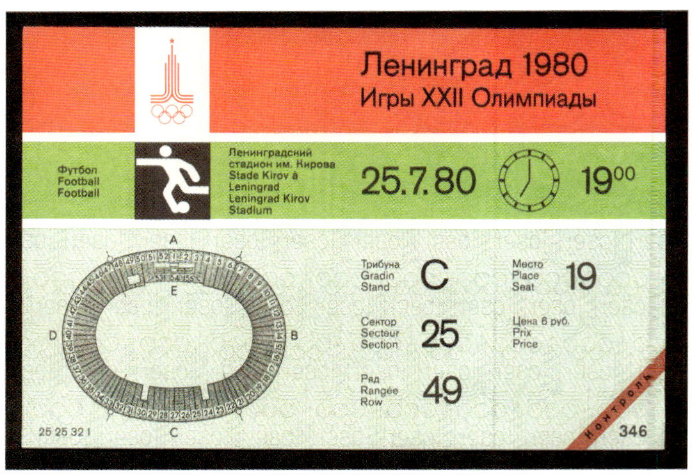

1980, Moscow. Single admission ticket, $20-25.

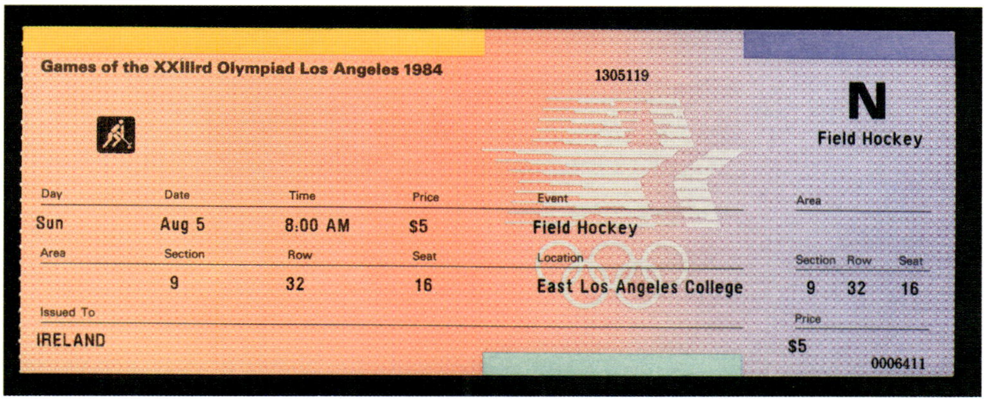

1984, Los Angeles. Single admission ticket, $10-15.

1984, Sarajevo. Single admission ticket, $30-40.

1988, Calgary. Single admission ticket, $15-20.

1988, Seoul. Single admission ticket, $20-25.

1992, Albertville. Single admission ticket, $10-15.

Year	City	Description	Rarity	Avg	Nr Mint
1994	Lillehammer	Single admission	5	$15	$20
1996	Atlanta	Single admission	5	$8	$10
1998	Nagano	Single admission	5	$10	$15
2000	Sydney	Single admission	5	$8	$10

[1]Prices are subjective due to extreme rarity.
[2]Code 217 printed on ticket
[3]Code 219 printed on ticket

1992, Barcelona. Single admission ticket, $15-20.

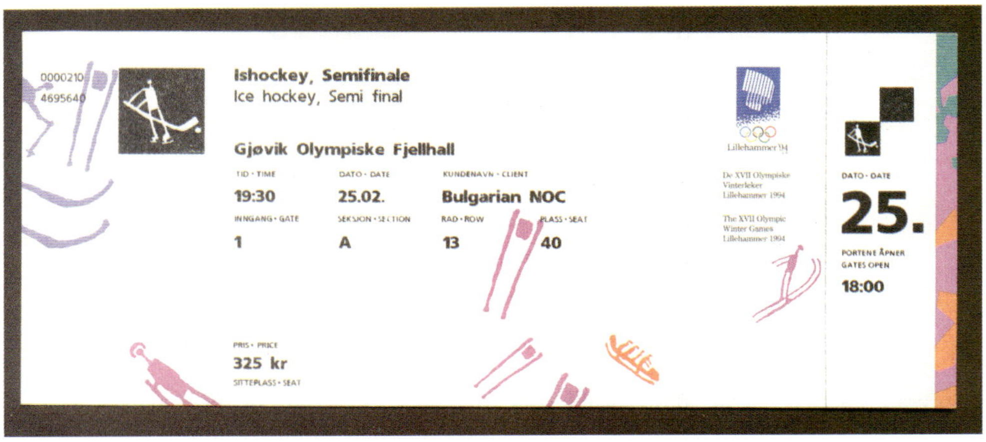

1994, Lillehammer. Single admission ticket, $15-20.

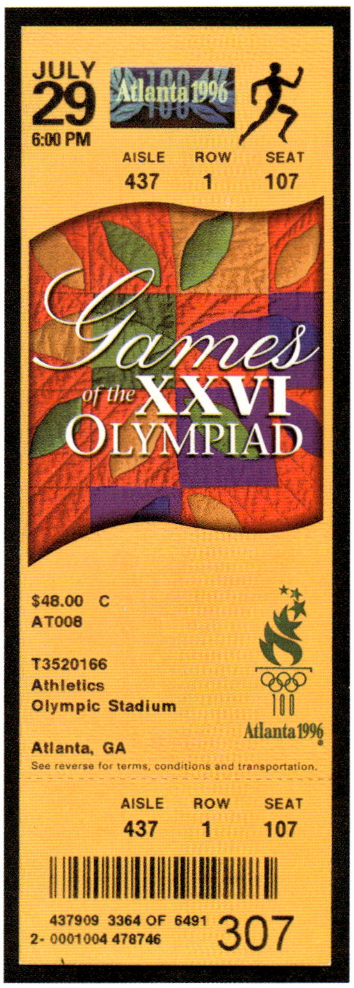

1996, Atlanta. Single admission ticket, $8-10.

2000, Sydney. Single admission ticket, $8-10.

1998, Nagano. Single admission ticket, $10-15.

OFFICIAL PRINTED MATERIAL

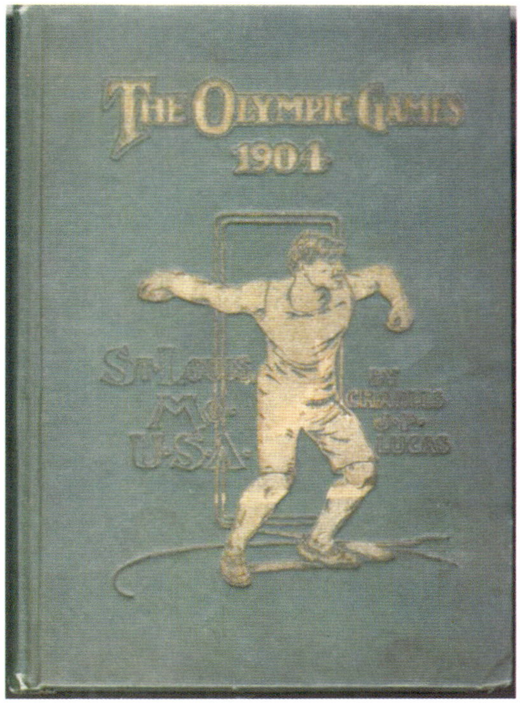

1904, St. Louis. Report: "The Olympic Games 1904" by Charles Lucas, $4000-5000.

Each of the Olympic Games produces volumes of printed matter in all shapes and sizes. While hundreds and hundreds of items are produced for each Olympics, both officially and unofficially, there are several items that are collected more than others. They include *Official Reports* which are publications produced by the organizing committee after the Olympic Games summarizing the entire event. *General Rules and Program* which are produced to help athletes and officials and *I.D.* cards which are issued to every athlete, official, and member of the press. Additionally, many of the larger National Olympic Committees produce their own official reports to summarize a specific Olympic Games and their country's involvement.

GRADING PRINTED MATERIAL

Printed material's condition is based on several factors, folds, tears, stains, foxing, and overall condition of the paper. If the material is in the form of a hardcover book, the condition of the binding is important.

Average Condition: Material may exhibit slight paper aging or foxing, minor creasing, or have minor professional restoration.

Near Mint Condition: Material should exhibit no writing, very minimal paper aging, no paper foxing, no stains and no restorations. If colored the coloring should be bright. If the material is bound the binding should be tight.

RARITY SCALE

See page 12.

Year	City	Description	Rarity	Avg	Nr Mint
1896	Athens	Official report	2	$3000	$3500
1900	Paris	Official report	1	$4000	$5000
1904	St. Louis	Official program of events	2	$1500	$1800
1904	St. Louis	Report: "Spalding's Official Athletic Almanac for 1905"	1	$4000	$5000
1904	St. Louis	Report: "The Olympic Games 1904" by Charle Lucas	1	$4000	$5000
1906	Athens	Official report	2	$900	$1200
1908	London	Official report	3	$600	$800
1912	Stockholm	Official report	4	$500	$700

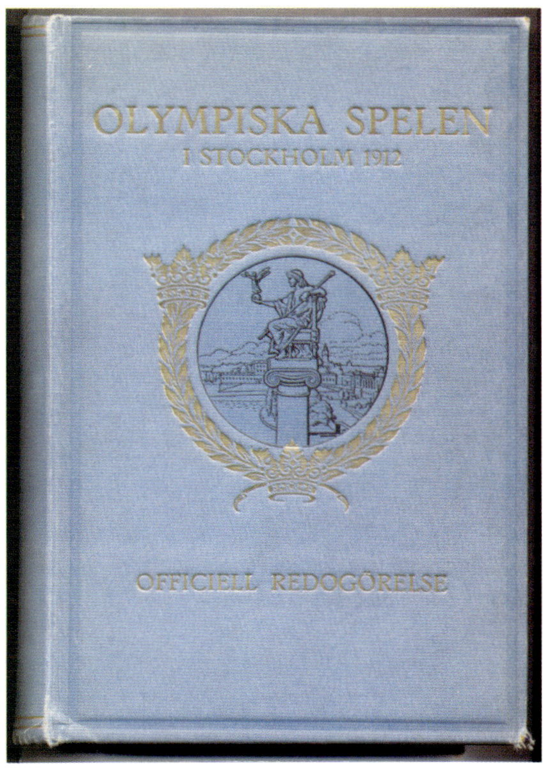

1912, Stockholm. Official report, $500-700.

Year	City	Description	Rarity	Avg	Nr Mint
1912	Stockholm	General rules and program	3	$100	$125
1920	Antwerp	Official report	1	$3000	$3500
1920	Antwerp	American Olympic Committee report	3	$150	$200
1920	Antwerp	General rules and program (booklets for each sport)	3	$125	$175
1920	Antwerp	I.D. card	2	$500	$600
1924	Chamonix	General rules and program	1	$1000	$1200
1924	Chamonix	I.D. card (same as Paris, 1924, but with winter athlete's name)	1	$350	$450
1924	Chamonix /Paris	American Olympic Committee report	2	$350	$450
1924	Chamonix /Paris	Official report	3	$700	$900
1924	Paris	I.D. card	3	$250	$450
1924	Paris	General rules and program (booklets for each sport)	3	$150	$175
1928	Amsterdam	I.D. card	3	$200	$275
1928	Amsterdam	General rules and program (booklets for each sport)	3	$125	$175
1928	Amsterdam	Official report	3	$400	$600
1928	St. Moritz	General rules and program	2	$250	$300
1928	St. Moritz	I.D. card	3	$300	$350
1928	St. Moritz	Preliminary booklet	3	$150	$175
1928	St. Moritz	Official results	2	$900	$1100

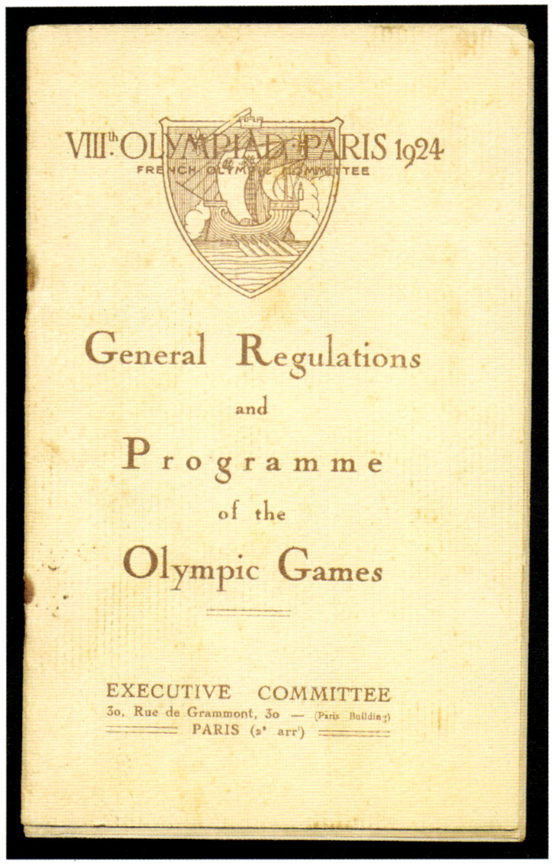

1924, Paris. General Rules and Program (general information), $150-200.

1924, Chamonix. General rules and program, $1000-1200.

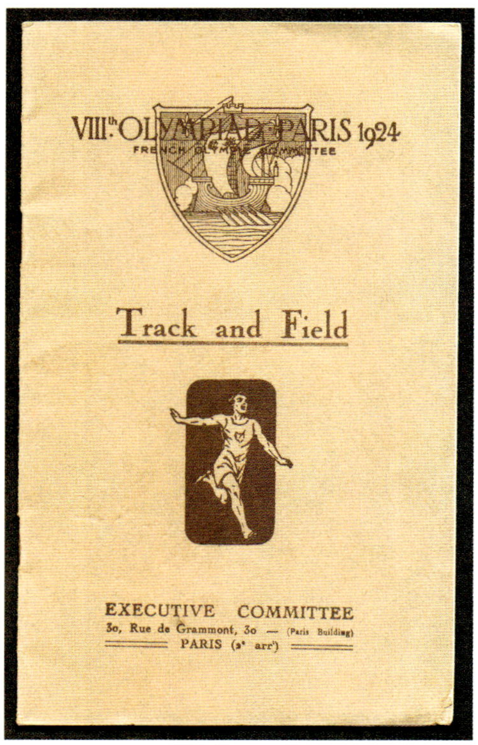

1924, Paris. General rules and program (booklets for each sport), $150-175.

1924, Paris/Chamonix. I.D. card, $250-450.

1928, St. Moritz. General rules and program, $250-300.

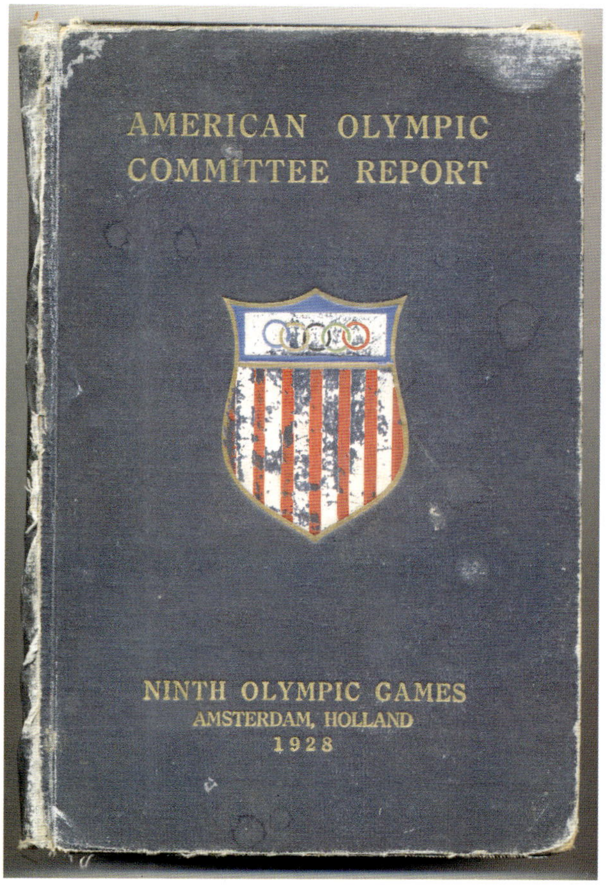

1928, St. Moritz/Amsterdam. American Olympic Committee report, $175-225.

1928, St. Moritz. Preliminary booklet, $150-175.

1932, Lake Placid. General rules and program, $125-175.

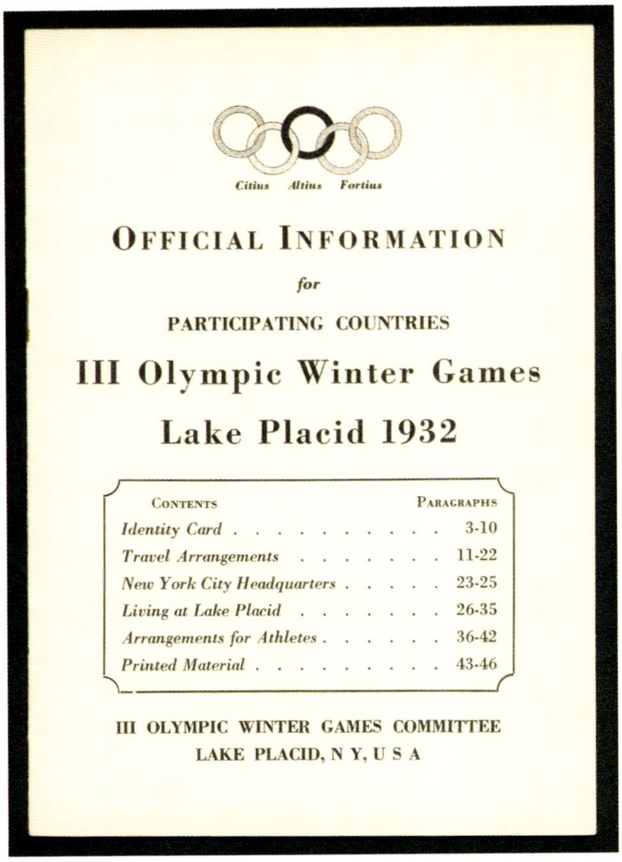

1932, Lake Placid. Official information for participating countries, $150-200.

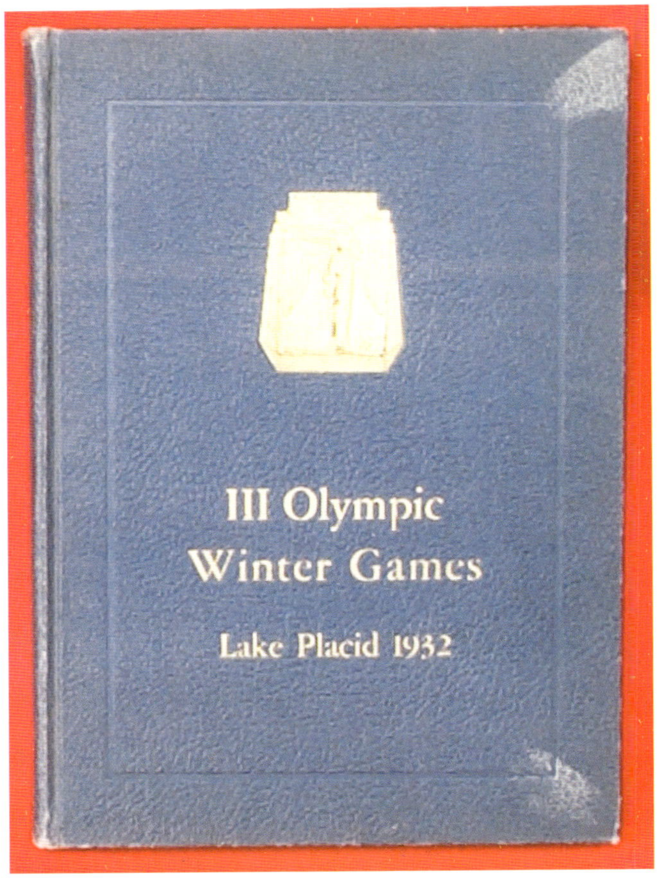

1932, Lake Placid. Official report, $300-375.

1932, Lake Placid. I.D. card, $250-300.

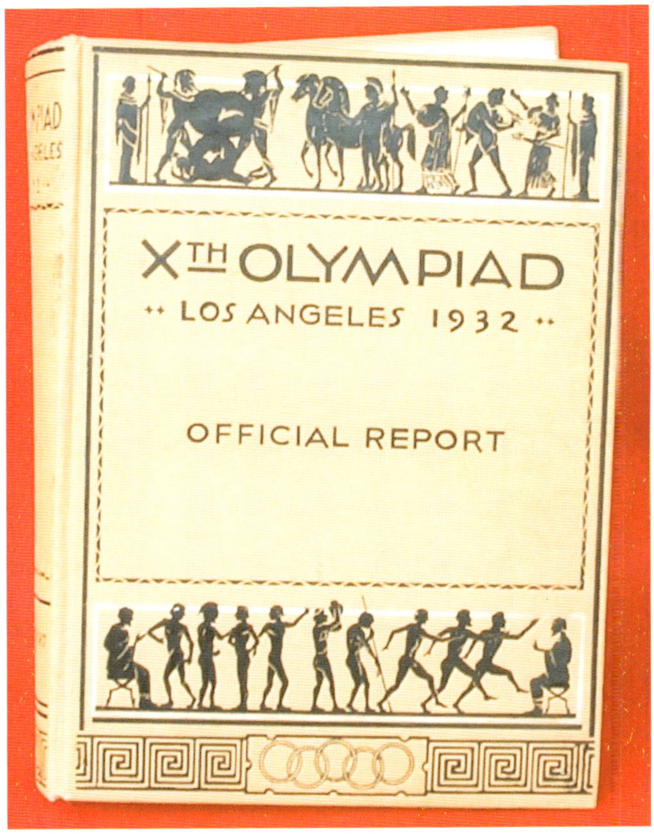

1932, Los Angeles. Official report (3 types of bindings), $400-800.

Year	City	Description	Rarity	Avg	Nr Mint
1960	Squaw Valley	I.D. wallet	3	$200	$250
1960	Squaw Valley	Official report	3	$300	$400
1960	Squaw Valley /Rome	U.S. Olympic Committee report	5	$25	$45
1964	Innsbruck	I.D. card	3	$150	$175
1964	Innsbruck	Official report	2	$800	$900
1964	Innsbruck	General rules and program	3	$125	$150
1964	Innsbruck/ Tokyo	U.S. Olympic Committee report	5	$20	$35
1964	Tokyo	Official report (2 volumes)	3	$400	$500
1964	Tokyo	I.D. card	4	$125	$150
1964	Tokyo	General rules and program (booklets for each sport)	4	$75	$100
1968	Grenoble	General rules and program	3	$125	$150
1968	Grenoble	I.D. card	4	$75	$100
1968	Grenoble	Official report	3	$600	$700
1968	Grenoble	I.D. wallet	4	$150	$175
1968	Grenoble /Mexico City	U.S. Olympic Committee report	5	$15	$25
1968	Mexico City	General rules and program (booklets for each sport)	4	$45	$55
1968	Mexico City	Official report (volume 5)	1	$2500	$3000
1968	Mexico City	Official report (volumes 1-4)	4	$300	$350
1968	Mexico City	I.D. wallet	4	$125	$150

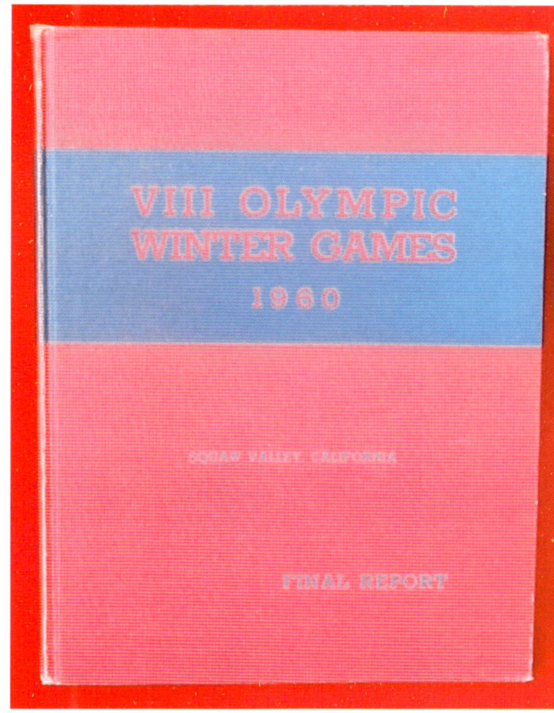

1960, Squaw Valley. Official report, $300-400.

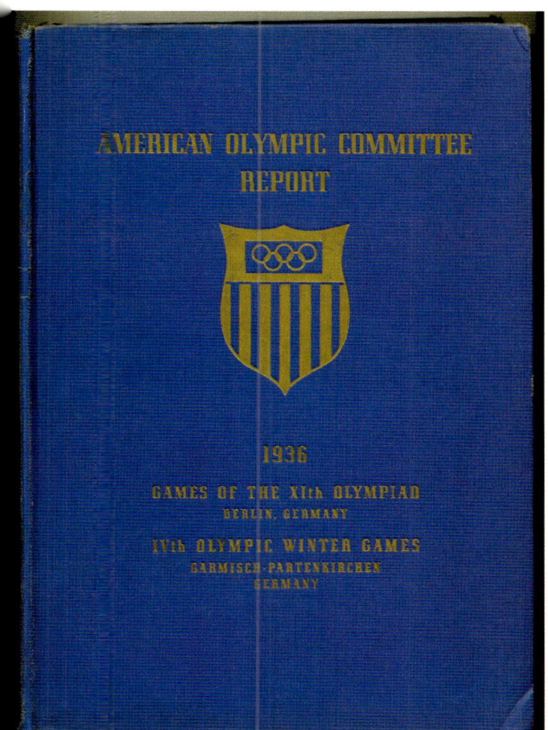

1936, Garmisch/Berlin. American Olympic Committee report, $125-175.

1968, Grenoble. I.D. wallet, $150-175.

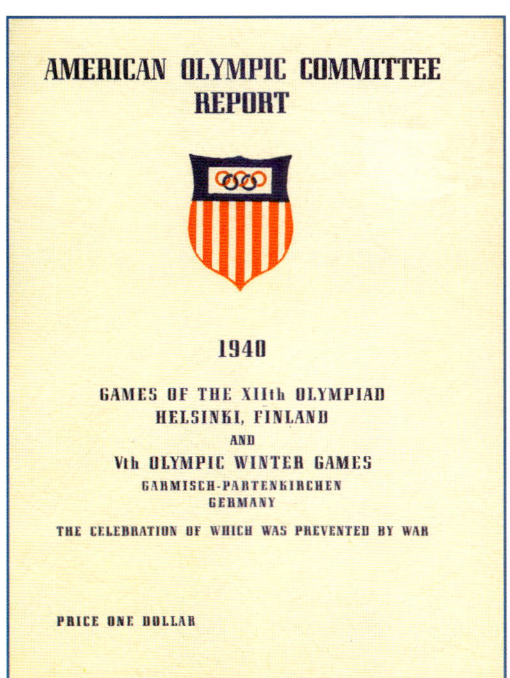

1940, Garmisch/Helsinki. American Olympic Committee report (games not held), $300-350.

Year	City	Description	Rarity	Avg	Nr Mint
1972	Munich	I.D. card	5	$75	$100
1972	Munich	Official report (3 volumes)	5	$200	$300
1972	Munich	General rules and program (booklets for each sport)	4	$35	$40
1972	Sapporo	Official report	3	$800	$900
1972	Sapporo	I.D. wallet	4	$150	$175
1972	Sapporo	General rules and program	3	$100	$125
1972	Sapporo /Munich	U.S. Olympic Committee report	5	$15	$25
1976	Innsbruck	General rules and program	3	$75	$100
1976	Innsbruck	I.D. card	4	$100	$125
1976	Innsbruck	Official report	4	$250	$300
1976	Innsbruck /Montreal	U.S. Olympic Committee report	5	$15	$25
1976	Montreal	General rules and program	5	$25	$30
1976	Montreal	I.D. card (plastic coated)	5	$75	$85
1976	Montreal	Official report (3 volumes)	4	$500	$600
1980	Lake Placid	I.D. card (plastic coated)	5	$50	$60
1980	Lake Placid	I.D. card (paper)	4	$100	$125
1980	Lake Placid	Official report (2 volumes)	5	$125	$175
1980	Lake Placid	General rules and program (booklets for each sport)	4	$30	$40
1980	Lake Placid /Moscow	U.S. Olympic Committee report	5	$15	$25
1980	Moscow	I.D. card (plastic coated)	5	$45	$55
1980	Moscow	Official report (3 volumes)	4	$300	$400
1980	Moscow	General rules and program (booklets for each sport)	5	$25	$30
1984	Los Angeles	Official report (2 volumes)	4	$500	$600
1984	Los Angeles	I.D. card (plastic coated)	5	$50	$60
1984	Los Angeles	General rules and program	5	$15	$20
1984	Sarajevo	General rules and program	4	$25	$30
1984	Sarajevo	Official report	4	$200	$250
1984	Sarajevo	I.D. card (plastic coated)	5	$65	$75
1984	Sarajevo /Los Angeles	U.S. Olympic Committee report	5	$10	$15
1988	Calgary	General rules and program (booklets for each sport)	5	$15	$20
1988	Calgary	Official report	4	$200	$250
1988	Calgary	I.D. card (plastic coated)	5	$50	$60
1988	Calgary/Seoul	U.S. Olympic Committee report	5	$10	$15
1988	Seoul	Official report (2 volumes)	4	$400	$500
1988	Seoul	General rules and program (booklets for each sport)	5	$10	$15
1988	Seoul	I.D. card (plastic coated)	5	$40	$50
1992	Albertville	I.D. card (plastic coated)	5	$50	$60
1992	Albertville	General rules and program (booklets for each sport)	4	$20	$25
1992	Albertville	Official report	4	$600	$700
1992	Albertville /Barcelona	U.S. Olympic Committee report	5	$10	$15
1992	Barcelona	I.D. card (plastic coated)	5	$40	$50
1992	Barcelona	Official report (volumes 1-4)	5	$300	$350
1992	Barcelona	Official report (volume 5, official results)	4	$300	$350
1992	Barcelona	General rules and program (booklets for each sport)	5	$10	$15
1994	Lillehammer	Official report (5 volumes)	4	$300	$400
1994	Lillehammer	I.D. card (plastic coated)	5	$40	$50
1994	Lillehammer	General rules and program (booklets for each sport)	5	$10	$15
1994	Lillehammer	U.S. Olympic Committee report	5	$10	$15
1996	Atlanta	I.D. card (plastic coated)	5	$25	$35
1996	Atlanta	Official report (3 volumes)	4	$300	$400
1996	Atlanta	General rules and program (booklets for each sport)	5	$10	$15
1996	Atlanta	U.S. Olympic Committee report	5	$10	$15
1998	Nagano	General rules and program (booklets for each sport)	5	$10	$15
1998	Nagano	U.S. Olympic Committee report	5	$10	$15
1998	Nagano	I.D. card (plastic coated)	5	$40	$50
1998	Nagano	Official report (3 volumes)	4	$600	$700
2000	Sydney	General rules and program (booklets for each sport)	5	$10	$15
2000	Sydney	I.D. card (plastic coated)	5	$25	$35

1972, Munich. Official report (3 volumes), $200-300.

1976, Innsbruck. Official report, $250-300.

1980, Lake Placid. I.D. card (plastic coated), $40-50.

1984, Sarajevo. I.D. card (plastic coated), $65-75.

1984, Los Angeles. I.D. card (plastic coated), $50-60.

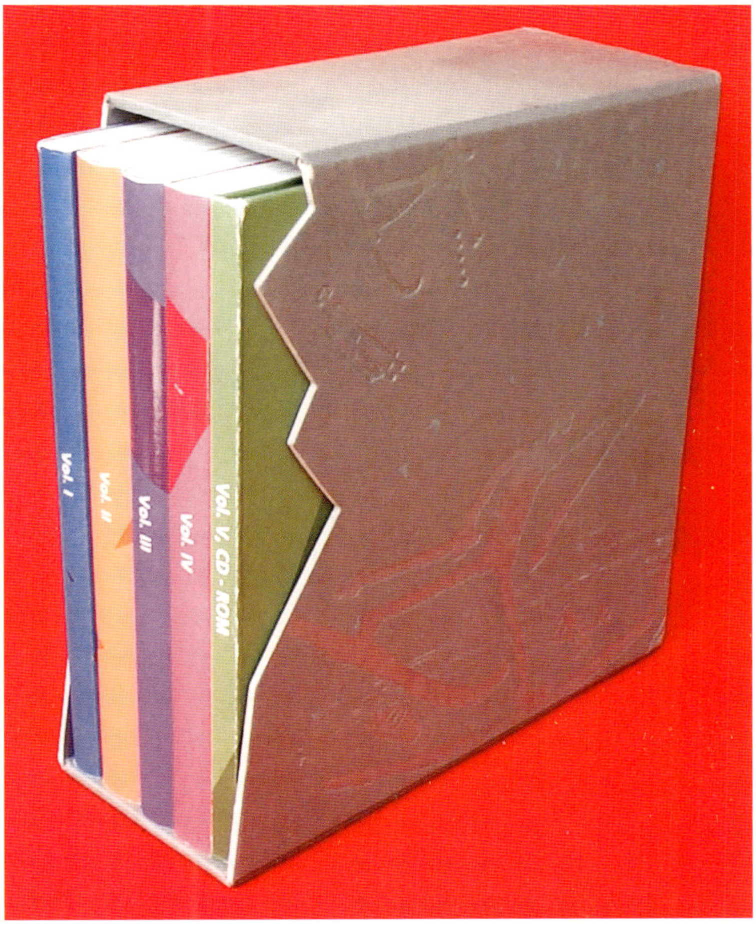

1994, Lillehammer. Official report (5 volumes), $300-400.

OLYMPIC PROGRAMS

Programs, both of the daily and souvenir type, have been popular at most sports events for years. Programs have been a part of the Olympic Games since 1896. The artwork on the covers of many Olympic programs is truly beautiful, and it comes in many artistic styles, spanning over a century of graphic design. Olympic programs are collected for their sports significance, information, and graphic design. In many games, daily programs have been produced for each sport, and have included both a schedule of events for that day, and a summary of results to that point. Souvenir programs are usually sold at the beginning of the Games and contain information of the events to be held, competitors, Olympic history, and a Games preview.

1904, St. Louis. Exposition daily program with Olympic references, $65-100.

GRADING OLYMPIC PROGRAMS

Programs are graded as most paper items are, by the condition of the paper, quality of the printing, and whether there are any marking, tears, folds, or creases. Usually scored programs aren't diminished in overall value, because scoring is evidence that the program was used during the event.

Average Condition: Minor edge and corner wear, slight creasing, some paper age or fading. No stains or folds.

Near Mint: Bright example with no folds, tears or creases. Bindings are tight. Minimal use with only the slightest hint of wear.

RARITY SCALE

See page 12

Some of the earliest programs Olympic programs are quite rare and valuable, such as 1896 or 1904. But most Olympic programs are available for $100 or less, making them very affordable. Winter Olympic programs are usually rarer than their Summer Olympic counterparts, but values seem to be consistent between summer and winter programs.

1924, Chamonix. Complete games program, $1000-1200.

Year	City	Description	Rarity	Avg	Nr Mint
1896	Athens	Daily program, no design on cover	1	$7500	$8000
1900	Paris	No Olympic programs known to exist			
1904	St. Louis	St. Louis Exposition daily program with Olympic references	3	$65	$100
1904	St. Louis	Official Olympic program with Teddy Roosevelt on the cover	1	$1200	$1800
1906	Athens	Daily program	2	$500	$600
1908	London	Franco-British Exposition daily program with Olympic references	3	$150	$200
1908	London	Olympic Games daily program	2	$300	$400
1912	Stockholm	Daily program with stadium and logo on cover	4	$100	$125
1920	Antwerp	Daily program with official poster on cover	2	$200	$300
1924	Chamonix	Complete games program	1	$1000	$1200
1924	Chamonix	Daily start sheet	1	$200	$250
1924	Paris	Daily program with official poster on cover	2	$150	$250
1928	Amsterdam	Daily program	4	$70	$90
1928	St. Moritz	Daily program	3	$150	$200

1928, Amsterdam. Daily program, $70-90.

1924, Paris. Daily program with official poster on cover, $150-250.

1928, St. Moritz. Daily program, $150-200.

Year	City	Description	Rarity	Avg	Nr Mint
1932	Lake Placid	Daily program	3	$75	$100
1932	Lake Placid	Souvenir Program	3	$75	$125
1932	Los Angeles	Daily program	5	$40	$50
1936	Berlin	Daily program	4	$40	$60
1936	Garmisch	Daily program	3	$150	$175

1932, Lake Placid. Daily program, $75-100.

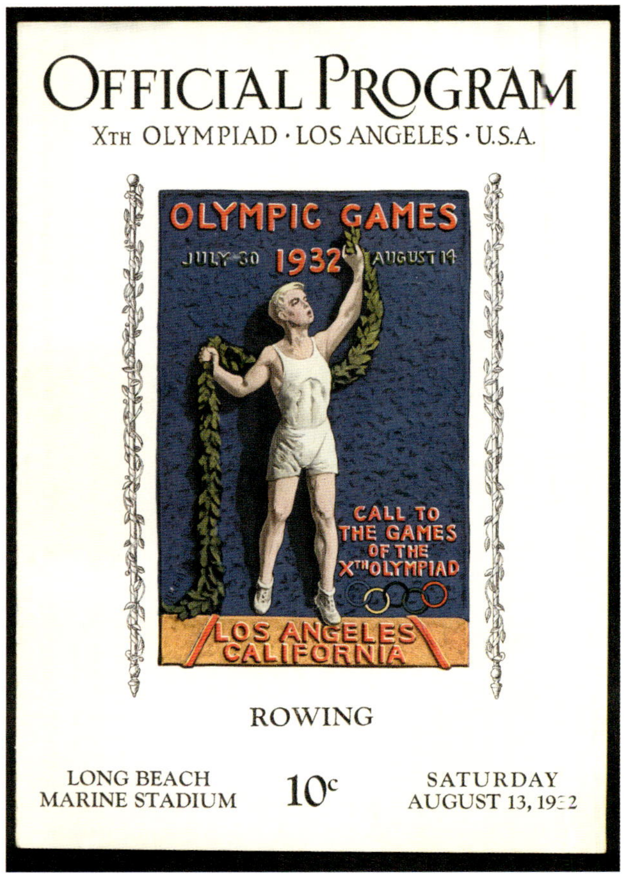

1932, Los Angeles. Daily program, $40-50.

1932, Lake Placid. Souvenir program, $75-125.

1936, Garmisch. Daily program, $150-175.

Year	City	Description	Rarity	Avg	Nr Mint
1948	London	Daily program	5	$25	$30
1948	London	Opening ceremonies program	4	$50	$70
1948	London	Souvenir program	4	$35	$50
1948	St. Moritz	Daily program	3	$75	$100
1952	Helsinki	Daily program	5	$25	$30
1952	Oslo	Daily program	4	$65	$75
1956	Cortina	Daily program	4	$65	$75

1948, London. Daily program, $25-30.

1952, Oslo. Daily program, $65-75.

1948, St. Moritz. Daily program, $75-100.

1956, Cortina. Daily program, $65-75.

Year	City	Description	Rarity	Avg	Nr Mint
1956	Melbourne	Daily program	5	$20	$25
1956	Melbourne	Opening ceremonies program	4	$35	$50
1960	Rome	Daily program	5	$30	$40
1960	Squaw Valley	Daily program	4	$60	$75
1960	Squaw Valley	Souvenir program	4	$50	$65
1964	Innsbruck	Daily program	4	$50	$75

1956, Melbourne. Daily program, $20-25.

1956, Stockholm. Equestrian events official program, $50-65.

1960, Squaw Valley. Souvenir program, $50-65.

1964, Innsbruck. Daily program, $50-75.

Year	City	Description	Rarity	Avg	Nr Mint
1964	Tokyo	Daily program	4	$65	$75
1968	Grenoble	No daily programs known			
1968	Mexico City	Daily program	4	$30	$35
1972	Munich	Daily program	5	$30	$35
1972	Sapporo	Daily program	3	$75	$85
1976	Innsbruck	Daily program	4	$50	$65
1976	Montreal	Daily start sheet	4	$5	$10
1976	Montreal	Event program	4	$25	$30
1980	Lake Placid	Closing ceremonies program	4	$20	$30
1980	Lake Placid	Daily start sheet	4	$10	$15
1980	Lake Placid	Opening ceremonies program	4	$15	$25
1980	Lake Placid	Souvenir program	5	$10	$15

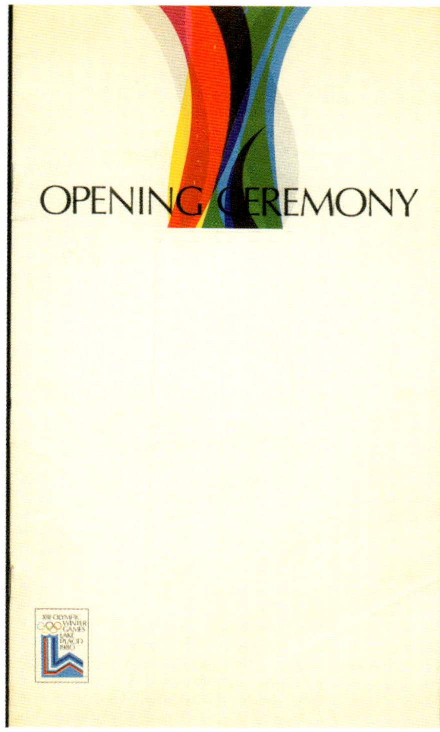

1980, Lake Placid. Opening ceremonies program, $15-25.

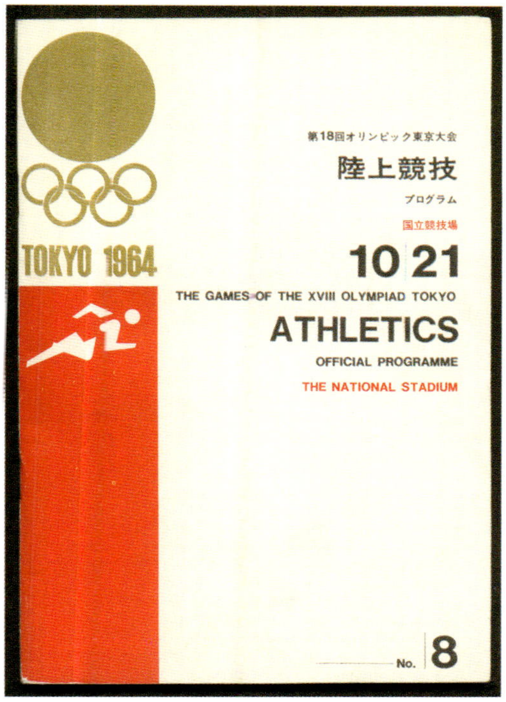

1964, Tokyo. Daily program, $65-75.

1980, Lake Placid. Souvenir program, $10-15.

1976, Innsbruck. Daily program, $50-65.

1992, Barcelona. Souvenir program, $15-20.

Year	City	Description	Rarity	Avg	Nr Mint
1980	Moscow	Daily program	4	$15	$20
1984	Los Angeles	Closing Ceremonies program	5	$10	$15
1984	Los Angeles	Opening Ceremonies program	5	$10	$15
1984	Los Angeles	Souvenir program	5	$15	$20
1984	Sarajevo	Souvenir program	4	$15	$20
1988	Calgary	Closing ceremonies program	4	$25	$30
1988	Calgary	Daily start sheet	5	$5	$10
1988	Calgary	Opening ceremonies program	4	$25	$30
1988	Calgary	Souvenir program	5	$10	$15
1988	Seoul	Souvenir program	5	$10	$15

1996, Atlanta. Souvenir program, $10-15.

Year	City	Description	Rarity	Avg	Nr Mint
1992	Albertville	Souvenir program	4	$20	$25
1992	Barcelona	Closing ceremonies program	5	$25	$30
1992	Barcelona	Daily start sheet	5	$5	$10
1992	Barcelona	Opening ceremonies program	5	$25	$30
1992	Barcelona	Souvenir program	5	$15	$20
1994	Lillehammer	Closing ceremonies program	4	$15	$20
1994	Lillehammer	Daily start sheet	4	$10	$15
1994	Lillehammer	Opening ceremonies program	4	$15	$20
1994	Lillehammer	Souvenir program	5	$15	$20
1996	Atlanta	Closing ceremonies program	5	$10	$15
1996	Atlanta	Opening ceremonies program	5	$10	$15
1996	Atlanta	Souvenir program	5	$10	$15
1998	Nagano	Closing ceremonies program	5	$20	$25
1998	Nagano	Daily start sheets	5	$5	$10
1998	Nagano	Opening ceremonies program	5	$20	$25
1998	Nagano	Souvenir program	5	$10	$15
2000	Sydney	Closing ceremonies program	5	$10	$15
2000	Sydney	Daily program	5	$5	$10
2000	Sydney	Opening ceremonies program	5	$10	$15
2000	Sydney	Souvenir program	5	$5	$10

1998, Nagano. Opening ceremonies program, $20-25.

DIPLOMAS

Olympic diplomas are paper certificates that are presented to both Olympic winners and participants. The designs of the diplomas are truly unique, and early diplomas are especially large, with wonderful graphics reflecting the era in which they were made. International Olympic rules state that a certain number of finishers in each event should receive a diploma. Also, each athlete and official should receive a participant diploma as well.

Originally, only medal winners received diplomas. The number of recipients was gradually expanded. In current Olympic Games, the first 8 places receive winner's diplomas. In most of the early Olympic Games, the design of the diplomas was the same, whether a winner or participant. Gradually, two designs were produced in most Olympics, one for the winner's diploma and one for the participant.

1904, St. Louis. St. Louis Exposition award diploma, $1500-2000.

GRADING DIPLOMAS

Diplomas are usually graded like most printed material. Take into account the condition of the paper, any folds, tears, staining, foxing, or visible restoration. Professionally mounting a diploma on linen does not decrease value, and can actually increase it.

Average Condition: Diploma may exhibit slight paper loss but not to the image, paper aging, or some non extensive restoration.

Near Mint: Diploma may exhibit extremely minor barely noticeable blemish or crease but no paper loss, minimal paper aging, minor restoration only to border not in the image.

RARITY SCALE

See page 12.

Year	City	Description	Rarity	Avg	Nr Mint
1896	Athens	Winner	1	$10000	$12000
1900	Paris	Winner	1	$2500	$3000
1904	St. Louis	St. Louis Exposition award diploma	3	$1500	$2000
1906	Athens	Winner	1	$3000	$3500
1908	London	Winner	2	$3500	$3800
1908	London	Participant	2	$2000	$2500
1912	Stockholm	Participant	2	$2500	$3000
1912	Stockholm	Winner	2	$3000	$3500

1912, Stockholm. Second place winner's diploma, $3000-3500.

Year	City	Description	Rarity	Avg	Nr Mint
1920	Antwerp	Winner	3	$2800	$3000
1920	Antwerp	Participant	3	$2200	$2400
1924	Chamonix	Winner	1	$6000	$6500
1924	Chamonix	Participant	1	$5000	$5500
1924	Paris	Participant	3	$2200	$2400
1924	Paris	Winner	3	$2000	$2500
1928	Amsterdam	Winner	3	$2800	$3000
1928	Amsterdam	Participant	3	$2000	$2400
1928	St. Moritz	Participant	2	$2000	$2500

1920, Antwerp. Participant's diploma, $2200-2400.

1928, Amsterdam. Participant's diploma, $2000-2400.

1924, Paris. Participant's diploma, $2200-2400.

1928, St. Moritz. Participant's diploma, $2000-2500.

Year	City	Description	Rarity	Avg	Nr Mint
1928	St. Moritz	Winner	2	$2500	$3500
1932	Lake Placid	Winner	3	$2000	$2500
1932	Lake Placid	Participant	3	$2000	$2500
1932	Lcs Angeles	Winner	3	$1800	$2500
1932	Lcs Angeles	Participant	3	$1400	$1800
1936	Berlin	Participant	3	$1800	$2000
1936	Berlin	Winner	3	$2500	$3000
1936	Garmisch	Winner	3	$3500	$4000
1936	Garmisch	Participant	3	$2000	$2500
1948	London	Winner	4	$700	$750
1948	London	Participant	4	$600	$650
1948	St. Moritz	Participant	4	$350	$375
1948	St. Moritz	Winner	3	$700	$800

1948, London. Participant's diploma, $600-650.

1932, Lake Placid. Winner's diploma, $2000-2500.

1948, St. Moritz. Winner's diploma, $700-800.

1932, Lcs Angeles. Participant's diploma, $1400-1800.

Year	City	Description	Rarity	Avg	Nr Mint
1952	Helsinki	Participant	4	$400	$450
1952	Helsinki	Winner	3	$500	$550
1952	Oslo	Winner	3	$700	$900
1952	Oslo	Participant	4	$275	$300
1956	Cortina	Participant	4	$300	$350
1956	Cortina	Winner	3	$800	$1000
1956	Melbourne	Participant	4	$200	$300
1956	Melbourne	Winner	4	$400	$500
1960	Rome	Winner	4	$800	$1000
1960	Rome	Participant	4	$300	$400
1960	Squaw Valley	Participant	3	$300	$400
1960	Squaw Valley	Winner	3	$600	$700
1964	Innsbruck	Participant	4	$300	$400
1964	Innsbruck	Winner	4	$600	$700
1964	Tokyo	Winner	4	$500	$550
1964	Tokyo	Participant	4	$200	$300
1968	Grenoble	Winner	4	$500	$600
1968	Grenoble	Participant	4	$200	$250
1968	Mexico City	Participant	5	$150	$175
1968	Mexico City	Winner	4	$500	$600
1972	Munich	Winner	5	$400	$500
1972	Munich	Participant	5	$75	$100
1972	Sapporo	Participant	4	$300	$400
1972	Sapporo	Winner	4	$600	$700
1976	Innsbruck	Participant	4	$200	$250
1976	Innsbruck	Winner	4	$500	$600
1976	Montreal	Winner	4	$500	$600
1976	Montreal	Participant	5	$125	$150
1980	Lake Placid	Participant	5	$50	$75
1980	Lake Placid	Winner	4	$400	$500
1980	Moscow	Winner	4	$400	$450
1980	Moscow	Participant	5	$75	$100
1984	Los Angeles	Participant	5	$100	$125
1984	Los Angeles	Winner	5	$500	$600
1984	Sarajevo	Participant	4	$300	$325
1984	Sarajevo	Winner	4	$1400	$1500
1988	Calgary	Winner	4	$500	$550
1988	Calgary	Participant	5	$175	$200
1988	Seoul	Participant	5	$100	$125
1988	Seoul	Winner	5	$450	$500
1992	Albertville	Participant	4	$125	$150
1992	Albertville	Winner	4	$400	$500
1992	Barcelona	Winner	5	$300	$400
1992	Barcelona	Participant	5	$75	$100
1994	Lillehammer	Participant	5	$150	$175
1994	Lillehammer	Winner	5	$300	$350
1996	Atlanta	Winner	5	$325	$350
1996	Atlanta	Participant	5	$75	$100
1998	Nagano	Participant	5	$100	$125
1998	Nagano	Winner	4	$300	$400
2000	Sydney	Participant	5	$50	$75
2000	Sydney	Winner	5	$200	$300

1952, Helsinki. Participant's diploma, $400-450.

1964, Innsbruck. Participant's diploma, $300-400.

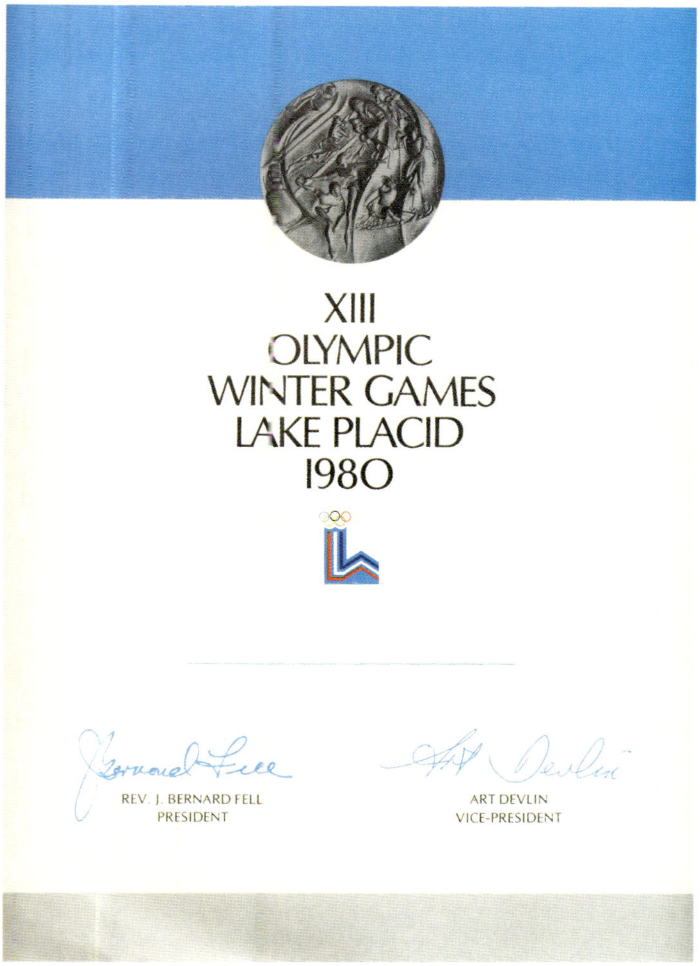

1980, Lake Placid. Participant's diploma, $50-75.

1996, Atlanta. Winner's diploma, $325-350.

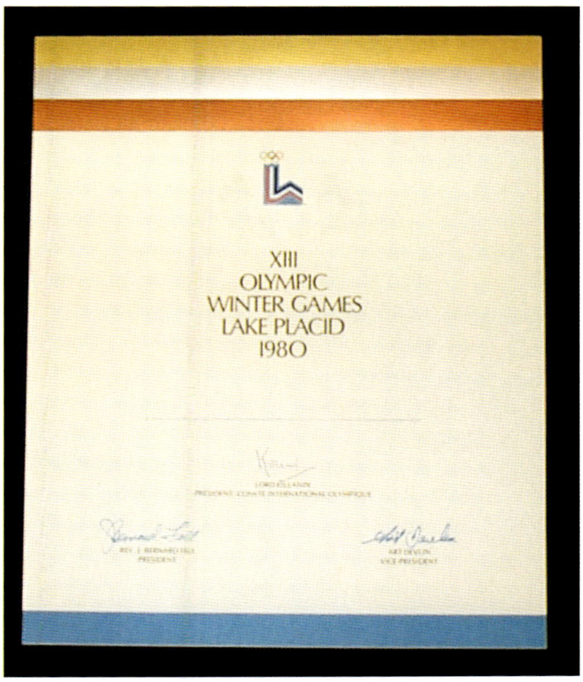

1980, Lake Placid. Winner's diploma, $400-500.

OLYMPIC POSTERS

The Modern Olympics were revived in 1896 and posters were used to promote the Games from the very beginning. It wasn't until the 1912 Stockholm Games that the first "official" Olympic poster was produced. It consisted of a striking design of a male athlete in the foreground surrounded by the flags of the competing nations. The poster was printed in 16 languages and in 3 sizes. This started a tradition that has continued and expanded. While only one type of poster was created for the 1912 Games, more recent Games have seen literally dozens of types produced. Originally, Olympic posters were a much-needed vehicle for advertising. Since print advertising was the only readily available medium for promoting the early Games through the late 1920s, posters were affixed to walls, displayed in windows of shops, and exhibited in numerous train stations all over the world. In the late 1960s and early 1970s Olympic posters began a new life as a moneymaker for Olympic Games organizers. The explosive growth of different styles of posters had begun. Many Olympic posters are beautiful works of art, and while some are quite common, they are still very collectible. Posters from the early years of the Games are very rare and valuable.

GRADING OLYMPIC POSTERS

Olympic posters, like any posters, are normally graded on a scale of "A" through "D." The "A" category is a poster in almost mint condition and the "D" category is a poster in poor condition. For this chapter, we are only rating Olympic posters from the "A" category and the "B" category (while not "almost mint" the poster is in good average condition). Please keep in mind that professionally mounting a poster on linen or Japan paper does not detract from the value. However, do not have a poster mounted on foam core or cardboard. This can severely damage the poster and lower the value substantially.

B Average Condition: Poster may exhibit slight paper loss but not to the image, paper aging, or some non extensive restoration.

A Near Mint: Poster may exhibit extremely minor, barely noticeable blemish or crease, but no paper loss, minimal paper aging, or minor restoration only to border not in the image.

RARITY SCALE

See page 12

The rarity of Olympic posters is a combination of quantity produced and age. Until the 1970s when Olympic posters became a true moneymaker for the games organizers, most posters were discarded or lost after an Olympics were concluded. Early posters can be worth substantially more than modern issues. Certain posters, such as recent Olympic "art series" posters, can be worth more to art collectors than to Olympic collectors.

Year	City	Description	Rarity	Avg	Nr Mint
1900	Paris	Female fencer holding three weapons	2	$3000	$3500
1912	Stockholm	Official emblem of the games, large size	3	$2500	$3000
1912	Stockholm	Official emblem of the games, small size	3	$1200	$1800
1920	Antwerp	Discus thrower over city, small size	3	$700	$1200
1920	Antwerp	Discus thrower over city, large size	2	$2500	$3500
1924	Chamonix	Bobsledders w/ eagle overhead	2	$3500	$4000
1924	Paris	Javelin thrower	2	$3000	$3800
1924	Paris	Saluting Athletes	2	$3000	$3500
1928	Amsterdam	Runner with Olympic Stadium in background, small size	2	$3000	$5000
1928	Amsterdam	Runner with Olympic Stadium in background, large size	1	$8000	$15000

1924, Paris. Saluting athletes under "Paris 1924", $3000-3500.

1900, Paris. Female fencer holding three weapons, $3000-3500.

1928, Amsterdam. Runner with the Olympic stadium in the background, large version, $8000-15000.

1912, Stockholm. Official emblem of the games, large size, $2500-3000.

Year	City	Description	Rarity	Avg	Nr Mint
1928	St. Moritz	Flags over the Alps	3	$2500	$3500
1932	Lake Placid	Ski jumper over a map of the United States	3	$2500	$3500
1932	Lake Placid	Bobsledders	4	$2000	$2500
1932	Los Angeles	Athlete with victory garland	3	$3000	$3500
1936	Berlin	Boats sailing at Kiel	2	$3500	$4000
1936	Berlin	Athlete over the Brandenburg Gate	3	$2500	$3500
1936	Berlin	Olympic torch relay map	2	$3000	$4000
1936	Berlin	Quadriga on top of Brandenburg Gate	2	$3000	$4000
1936	Garmisch	Saluting athlete	3	$2500	$3500
1940	Helsinki (not held)	Runner over map of Scandinavia	2	$2500	$3000
1948	London	Discus thrower in front of Big Ben, small size	3	$700	$1000
1948	London	Discus thrower in front of Big Ben, medium size	3	$800	$1200
1948	London	Discus thrower in front of Big Ben, large size	2	$3000	$4000
1948	St. Moritz	Two skiers looking at the rising sun	3	$2000	$2500
1948	St. Moritz	Skier, hands raised, over the alps	3	$2000	$2500
1948	St. Moritz	Alpine mountain lake with Games logo	3	$2000	$2500
1948	St. Moritz	Smiling sun over alpine mountain	3	$2000	$2500

1932, Lake Placid. Ski jumper over a map of the United States, $2500-3500.

1928, St. Moritz. Flags over the Alps, $2500-3500.

1932, Los Angeles. Athlete with victory garland, $3000-3500.

1936, Berlin. Athlete over the Brandenburg Gate, $2500-3500.

1948, London. Discus thrower in front of Big Ben, large version, $3000-4000.

1936, Garmisch. Saluting athlete, $2500-3500.

1948, St. Moritz. Skier, with hands raised, over the alps, $2000-2500.

Year	City	Description	Rarity	Avg	Nr Mint
1952	Helsinki	Runner over map of Scandinavia (similar to 1940), small size	4	$400	$600
1952	Helsinki	Runner over map of Scandinavia similar to 1940), large size	3	$1500	$1800
1952	Oslo	Athlete raising the Olympic flag	3	$1500	$1800
1952	Oslo	Ski poles, each with flag attached	3	$2000	$2500
1956	Cortina	Olympic torch in front of the Dolomite Mountains	2	$1800	$2200
1956	Cortina	Official logo poster	3	$1500	$2000
1956	Melbourne	Olympic rings over Melbourne city seal, large size	4	$900	$1400
1956	Melbourne	Olympic rings over Melbourne city seal, small size	4	$400	$600
1956	Stockholm	Horse and rider	3	$2500	$3000
1960	Rome	Roman column with she-wolf at the top	4	$500	$800
1960	Squaw Valley	Official logo poster	3	$500	$800
1960	Squaw Valley	Slalom flag with map of U.S.	4	$400	$600
1964	Innsbruck	Large section of a snowflake with the Olympic rings	3	$700	$1000
1964	Tokyo	Official logo poster	3	$800	$1200
1964	Tokyo	Torch relay runner over logo	3	$800	$1200
1964	Tokyo	Runners at the start of a race	3	$800	$1200
1964	Tokyo	Swimmer doing butterfly stroke	3	$800	$1200
1968	Grenoble	Reverse silhouette of torch, overview of Grenoble	3	$400	$600
1968	Grenoble	Flags	3	$300	$500
1968	Grenoble	Large Olympic rings moving downhill	3	$400	$600
1968	Grenoble	Venue series, pictures of competition sites	3	$150	$300
1968	Grenoble	Official logo poster, small size	3	$500	$600
1968	Mexico City	Sports series, depiction of various events	4	$75	$100
1968	Mexico City	Aztec Calendar	4	$100	$150
1968	Mexico City	Geometric design with "Mexico 68" in center	4	$100	$150
1972	Munich	View of tent-like roofs of venues, Olympic TV tower	4	$75	$125
1972	Munich	Sport series, nine different sports posters	5	$40	$65
1972	Munich	Art series, 16 different posters	4	$75	$150
1972	Sapporo	Figure skater	3	$400	$600
1972	Sapporo	Smaller logo poster	3	$400	$600
1972	Sapporo	Downhill skier	3	$400	$600
1972	Sapporo	Large logo poster	3	$400	$600
1976	Innsbruck	Official logo poster	4	$150	$350
1976	Innsbruck	Elderly skier	3	$250	$400
1976	Montreal	Three views of the Olympic stadium, large and small sizes	5	$20	$25
1976	Montreal	Amik, beaver mascot, large and small sizes	5	$20	$25
1976	Montreal	Montreal logo flag, large and small sizes	5	$20	$25
1976	Montreal	Sports series	5	$20	$25
1976	Montreal	Olympic rings in motion, large and small sizes	5	$20	$25
1980	Lake Placid	US and Olympic flags in front of mountain	5	$30	$50
1980	Lake Placid	Sports series 1, athletes in 7 colors	5	$25	$35
1980	Lake Placid	Mascots competing in 13 sports	5	$25	$35
1980	Lake Placid	Sports series 2, athletes in monochrome	5	$20	$30
1980	Lake Placid	Official logo poster	5	$15	$25
1980	Moscow	Assorted styles	5	$20	$25
1980	Moscow	Official logo poster	5	$20	$25

1960, Squaw Valley. Slalom flag with map of the United States, $400-600.

1964, Tokyo. Runner with the Olympic torch, $800-1200.

1972, Munich. View of tent-like roofs of venues, Olympic TV tower, $75-125.

1976, Innsbruck. Official logo poster, $150-350.

1980, Lake Placid. US and Olympic flags in front of a mountain, $30-50.

1972, Sapporo. Large logo poster, $400-600.

1976, Montreal. Amik, the beaver mascot, both large and small version, $20-25.

1980, Moscow. Mascot holding winner's medals and flowers, $20-25.

Year	City	Description	Rarity	Avg	Nr Mint
1984	Los Angeles	Official logo poster	5	$40	$50
1984	Los Angeles	Art series	4	$50	$75
1984	Sarajevo	Official logo poster	4	$75	$125
1984	Sarajevo	Mascot with skis	4	$75	$125
1984	Sarajevo	Sports series, watercolors of athletes in action, large and small	4	$75	$125
1984	Sarajevo	Art series	4	$50	$75
1988	Seoul	Mascot, small size	5	$50	$75
1988	Seoul	Mascots depicting many sports	5	$75	$100
1988	Seoul	Torch relay, large size	5	$75	$100
1988	Seoul	Torch relay, small size	5	$50	$75
1988	Seoul	Mascot, large size	5	$75	$100
1988	Seoul	Official logo poster	5	$75	$100
1992	Albertville	Mascot, small size	4	$35	$45
1992	Albertville	Mascot, large size	4	$50	$75
1992	Albertville	Aerial view of venue sites	4	$45	$55
1992	Albertville	Official emblem poster	4	$75	$90
1992	Barcelona	Sports series	5	$20	$25
1992	Barcelona	Mosaic series	5	$20	$25
1994	Lillehammer	Mascots	4	$65	$80
1994	Lillehammer	Pictogram series	4	$65	$80
1996	Atlanta	Official bid logo	4	$25	$35
1996	Atlanta	Official logo poster	5	$20	$25
1998	Nagano	Official logo poster	5	$20	$30
1998	Nagano	Mascots	5	$20	$30
2000	Sydney	Sports series	5	$8	$10
2000	Sydney	Mascot series	5	$10	$14
2000	Sydney	Official logo poster	5	$8	$10

1992, Albertville. Official emblem design, $75-90.

1992, Barcelona. Hands showing "v" for victory, $20-25.

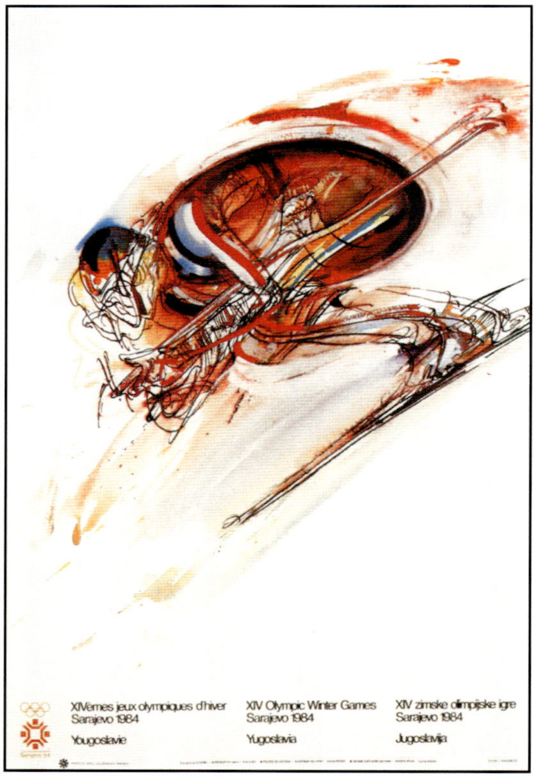

1984, Sarajevo. From the sports series, downhill skier, both large and small version, $75-125.

1988, Seoul. Torch relay runner, large version, $75-100.

1996, Atlanta. Graphic design with the official logo at the bottom, $20-25.

OLYMPIC MASCOTS

The word "mascot" goes back to the middle of the 19th century and has French origins. Although unofficial, the first Olympic mascot appeared in Grenoble, France at the 1968 winter games. "Schuss" was a character with a large head and was portrayed on skis. Four years later the first official Olympic mascot was "Waldi" the Dachshund seen at the 1972 Munich, Germany summer games. "Waldi started the tradition." Since 1972 every Olympic city has been represented by a mascot or mascots. The first dual mascots arrived at the Calgary, Canada, winter games. Polar bear siblings "Hidy" and "Howdy" were the "talk of the town" in 1988. Multiple mascots hit the Olympic scene in Nagano, Japan in 1998 with the four snow owls known as "Snowlets." Multiple mascots seem to have become the rage since. Olympic mascots have been portrayed as whimsical fantasy creations, cute and cuddly animals, and folklore characters. They have been produced in countless forms, including small toys, posters, stickers, patches, banks, key chains, plates, pins, and buttons. This chapter will focus on the most popular form of Olympic mascot – the colorful and enchanting plush toy.

GRADING OLYMPIC MASCOTS

Grading Olympic mascots is based on overall appearance of the plush toy. Newer mascots should always be in near mint condition.

Average condition: Signs of handling and possible slight fading of colors.

Near mint condition: Bright like new appearance with no fading.

RARITY SCALE

See page 12.

Year	City	Description	Rarity	Avg	Nr Mint
1968	Grenoble	"Schuss" – 13cm, terrycloth cartoon character on skis	1	$350	$400
1968	Grenoble	"Schuss – 11cm, plastic cartoon character on skis with Olympic rings on head	2	$210	$250
1968	Grenoble	"Schuss" – 9.5cm, plastic cartoon character on skis	3	$130	$220
1972	Munich	"Waldi" – 41cm, fabric stuffed Dachshund	3	$140	200
1972	Munich	"Waldi" – 20.5cm, velvet stuffed Dachshund	4	$120	$150
1972	Munich	"Waldi" – 27cm, multicolored velvet stuffed Dachshund	3	$145	$165
1972	Munich	"Waldi" – 52cm, multicolored linen stuffed Dachshund	2	$200	225
1972	Munich	"Waldi" – 25cm, rubber movable head and tail	3	$145	$160
1976	Innsbruck	"Schneemann" – 19.8cm, white felt covered hard body snowman	1	$380	$430
1976	Innsbruck	"Schneemann" - 11cm, white felt covered hard body snowman as hockey player	1	$350	$380
1976	Innsbruck	"Schneemann" – 25cm, inflatable snowman	3	$150	$175
1976	Innsbruck	"Sonnenweiberl" – 30.5cm, wife of mascot snowman	1	$380	$440
1976	Montreal	"Amik" – 43cm, plush toy beaver	1	$275	$325

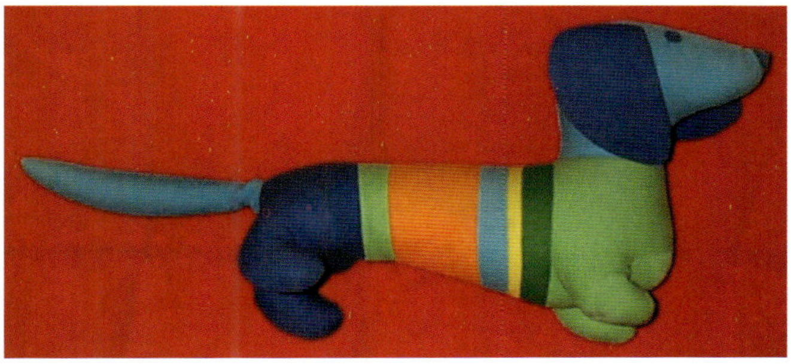

1972, Munich. "Waldi" – Fabric stuffed Dachshund mascot, $140-200.

1976, Montreal. "Amik" – Plush toy beaver mascot, $275-325.

Year	City	Description	Rarity	Avg	Nr Mint
1980	Lake Placid	"Roni" – 37cm, cloth covered toy raccoon	4	$40	$50
1980	Lake Placid	"Roni" – 55.5cm, plush toy raccoon	4	$65	$80
1980	Moscow	"Misha" – 30cm, plush toy bear	5	$25	$30
1980	Moscow	"Misha" – 34cm, plush toy bear	4	$30	$40
1980	Moscow	"Misha" – 34cm, plush, smiling, made in Russia	5	$55	$70
1980	Moscow	"Misha" – 20cm, plush covered yellow/brown foam	5	$35	$50
1980	Moscow	"Vigri" – 13.5cm, plush toy seal	2	$220	$270
1980	Moscow	"Vigri" – 19cm, felt covered foam seal	2	$200	$250
1980	Moscow	"Vigri – 21cm, plush covered green/yellow foam seal	2	$195	$235
1984	Sarajevo	"Vucko" – 22cm, plush toy wolf	3	$25	$35
1984	Sarajevo	"Vucko" – 20.5cm, plush toy wolf	4	$20	$25
1984	Sarajevo	"Vucko" – 62cm, plush toy wolf, made in Yugoslavia	2	$150	$200
1984	Los Angeles	"Sam" – 38cm, Plush toy eagle	4	$25	$35
1988	Calgary	"Hidy" and Howdy" – 25.5cm, plush toy polar bears (pair)	4	$80	$100
1988	Seoul	"Hodori" – 25cm, plush toy tiger (male)	5	$40	$50
1988	Seoul	"Hodori" – 32cm, plush toy tiger (male)	5	$50	$60
1992	Albertville	"Magique" – 26.5cm, plush toy snow imp	5	$50	$65
1992	Barcelona	"Cobi – 32cm, plush toy surreal dog	5	$64	$75
1994	Lillehammer	"Haakon" and "Kristin"–23cm, plush toy, folklore children (pr.)	5	$75	$100
1994	Lillehammer	"Haakon" and "Kristin" - 35.5cm, plush toy, folklore children (pair)	3	$180	$240
1996	Atlanta	"Whatizit" – 31.5cm, fantasy figure	4	$25	$35
1996	Atlanta	"Izzy" – 26.50cm, plush toy fantasy figure	5	$20	$30
1996	Atlanta	"Izzy" – 53cm, plush toy fantasy figure backpack	5	$30	$45
1998	Nagano	"Sukki," "Nokki," "Lekki," and "Tsukki" – 13cm, plush toy snow owls (set of 4)	5	$150	$180

1980, Moscow. "Misha" – Plush toy bear, $55-65.

1984, Sarajevo. "Vucko" – Plush toy wolf mascot, $25-35.

1980, Lake Placid. "Roni" – Plush raccoon mascot, $65-80.

1992, Albertville. "Magique" – Plush toy snow imp mascot, $50-65.

Year	City	Description	Rarity	Avg	Nr Mint
2000	Sydney	"Ollie" – plush toy kookaburra, "Syd" - plush toy platypus, and "Millie" – plush toy echidna (set of 3, all 10.6cm)	5	$65	$80
2000	Sydney	"Ollie" – plush toy kookaburra, "Syd" – plush toy platypus, and"Millie" – plush toy echidna (set of 3, all 12.7cm)	5	$60	$70

**Mascots with original tags and packaging will add a premium to certain collectors. This is especially true with older mascots.

2000, Sydney. "Ollie" – plush toy kookaburra, "Syd" – plush toy platypus(center right), and "Millie" – plush toy echidna (bottom left), mascots (set of 3), $60-70.

1992, Barcelona. "Cobi" – Plush toy surreal dog mascot, $64-75.

1994, Lillehammer. "Haakon" and "Kristin" – Plush toy, folklore children (pair) mascots, $75-100.

1998, Nagano. "Sukki, "Nokki," "Lekki," and "Tsukki" – Plush toy snow owls "Snowlets" (set of 4) mascots, $150-180.

MISCELLANEOUS OLYMPIC COLLECTIBLES

If you can think of any kind of unusual souvenir, the odds are that it was made for the Olympic Games at least once. Everything from cups, plates, and toys to ashtrays, lighters, paperweights, scarves, and so much more has been produced over the years. Both official and non-official items have been made. In the early years of the Olympics licensing was not really enforced and, during that period, the largest quantities of collectibles were produced. We have included in this chapter items that don't fall into any of our other chapters. They include items produced for official consumption by athletes and officials as well as general souvenirs available to the public. Please keep in mind that we have included only a representative sample of miscellaneous items as there are literally thousands of items from which to choose.

GRADING MISCELLANEOUS OLYMPIC COLLECTIBLES

It sometimes is more difficult to grade items that don't fall under a specific category. Check for wear and tear on the item in question. Also check the coloring for brightness. If the item is made of paper or cardboard check for folds or tears. Cracks in any glass, pottery, or porcelain object can significantly lower its value.

Average condition: Minor wear, fold, crease or fading. No cracks or chips in glassware.

Near mint condition: Almost out of the box condition. No folds, creases, cracks or chips. Colors are bright.

RARITY SCALE

See page 12

Year	City	Description	Rarity	Avg	Nr Mint
1900	Paris	Stereo view of gymnastics competition	2	$300	$400
1900	Paris	Souvenir map of exposition including Olympic venue	2	$175	$200
1900	Paris	Silk scarf with aerial view of Paris Exposition	4	$75	$100

1900, Paris. Stereo view of gymnastics competition, $300-400.

Year	City	Description	Rarity	Avg	Nr Mint
1904	St. Louis	Stereo view of Ralph Rose putting the shot	2	$800	$1,000
1904	St. Louis	Souvenir map of exposition including Olympic venue	3	$100	$125
1908	London	Various postcards of venues and events	3	$35	$55
1912	Stockholm	Various postcards	4	$20	$25
1912	Stockholm	Cotton handkerchief with Swedish flag & legend in corner	3	$125	$150
1912	Stockholm	Porcelain plate of the entrance to the Olympic stadium	3	$200	$225
1912	Stockholm	Porcelain plate of the Olympic stadium	3	$225	$250
1912	Stockholm	Silver-plate ashtray with games logo in center	4	$125	$150
1912	Stockholm	Souvenir cup or small vase with official logo in pewter	4	$100	$125
1920	Antwerp	Various postcards	3	$50	$75
1924	Paris	Various postcards	3	$45	$55
1928	Amsterdam	Porcelain plate of 6 views of Olympic events around city coat of arms	4	$225	$275
1928	Amsterdam	Brass octagonal charger	4	$175	$200
1928	Amsterdam	Porcelain plate of athlete and Olympic rings	3	$300	$350
1928	Amsterdam	Ceramic tile depicting Olympic cauldron and legend	4	$225	$250
1928	Amsterdam	Porcelain plate of Amsterdam coat of arms	3	$325	$375
1928	Amsterdam	Pocket knife	3	$125	$150
1928	Amsterdam	Porcelain plate of Olympic stadium and flame	3	$600	$650
1928	Amsterdam	Orange glass soccer ball with legend	4	$100	$125
1932	Lake Placid	Felt pennant in blue with Olympic rings	3	$150	$175

1912, Stockholm. Various postcards each, $20-25.

1924, Paris. Various postcards each, $45-55.

1908, London. Various postcards of venues and events, $35-55.

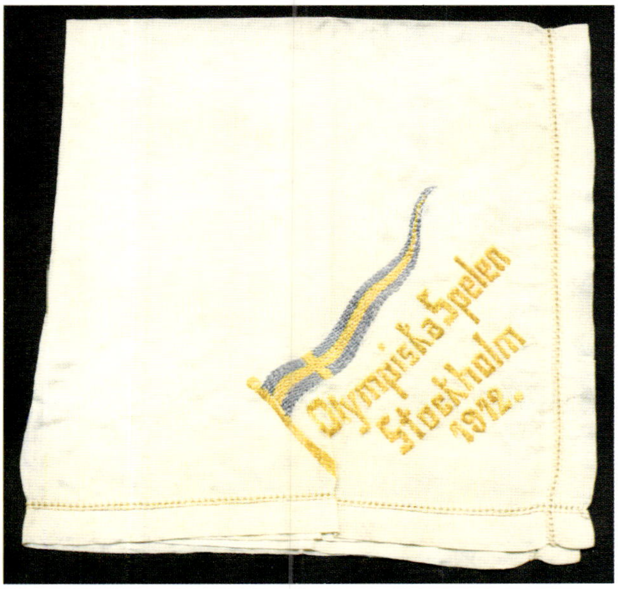

1912, Stockholm. Cotton handkerchief with Swedish flag & legend in corner, $125-150.

1932, Lake Placid. Large round souvenir blue felt patch with Olympic rings, $40-75.

Year	City	Description	Rarity	Avg	Nr Mint
1932	Lake Placid	Felt pennant in blue with figure skater and Olympic rings	3	$175	$200
1932	Lake Placid	Official diamond shaped patch with Olympic rings	3	$75	$100
1932	Lake Placid	Large round souvenir blue felt patch with Olympic rings	4	$40	$75
1932	Lake Placid	Felt pennant in orange with ski jumper and Olympic rings	3	$200	$225
1932	Lake Placid	Felt pennant in orange with Olympic rings	3	$150	$175
1932	Los Angeles	Bracelet made of 4 metal bangles with logo in center	4	$115	$125
1932	Los Angeles	Steel matchbox cover with discus thrower and L.A. Coliseum	4	$75	$95
1932	Los Angeles	Gold plated bracelet with Games logo in center	4	$135	$145
1932	Los Angeles	Die-cut cardboard puzzle depicting athletes with text & legend	4	$50	$75
1932	Los Angeles	Souvenir paper and wood parasol with games logo	3	$75	$100
1932	Los Angeles	Plaster model of the L.A. Coliseum	3	$100	$125
1932	Los Angeles	Cast white metal ashtray with local advertisement	4	$75	$95
1932	Los Angeles	Silver plated spoon with Olympic legend	4	$45	$55
1932	Los Angeles	Felt mini pennant in blue with white legend	3	$100	$120
1932	Los Angeles	Felt pennant in blue with circular legend and "X-Olympiad"	4	$125	$150

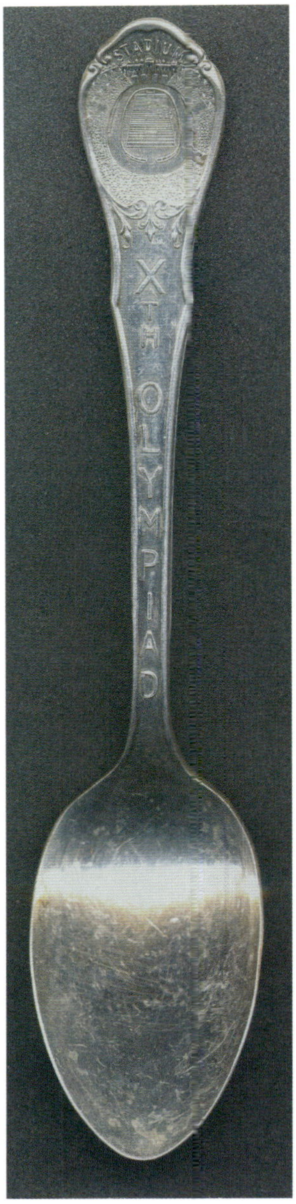

1932, Los Angeles. Silver-plated spoon with Olympic legend, $45-55.

1932, Lake Placid. Official diamond shaped patch with Olympic rings, $75-100.

1932, Los Angeles. Felt mini pennant in blue with white legend, $100-120.

1932, Los Angeles. Gold plated bracelet with Games logo in center, $135-145.

Year	City	Description	Rarity	Avg	Nr Mint
1932	Los Angeles	Souvenir paper and wood fan with scene of L.A. and games logo	4	$50	$65
1932	Los Angeles	Souvenir cushion of oiled canvas with discus thrower and legend	3	$125	$150
1932	Los Angeles	Coca-Cola circular paper events wheel	4	$75	$100
1936	Berlin	Silk handkerchief with Olympic rings surrounded by flags of competing nations	4	$65	$75
1936	Berlin	Small souvenir Olympic flag with ties and leather corners	4	$75	$100

1936, Berlin. Chrome and steel lighter with Olympic rings and Brandenburg Gate, $150-175.

1932, Los Angeles. Souvenir paper and wood fan with scene of L.A. and games logo, $50-65.

1936, Berlin. Silk handkerchief with Olympic rings surrounded by flags of competing nations, $65-75.

1932, Los Angeles. Steel matchbox cover with discus thrower and L.A. Coliseum, $75-95.

1936, Berlin. Small souvenir Olympic flag with ties and leather corners, $75-100.

Year	City	Description	Rarity	Avg	Nr Mint
1936	Berlin	Watch fob with Olympic bell, black ribbon and clip	4	$175	$195
1936	Berlin	Ashtray with etched design of a discus thrower in glass	4	$50	$65
1936	Berlin	Chrome and steel lighter with Olympic rings and Brandenburg Gate	4	$150	$175
1936	Berlin	Bakelite model of Olympic stadium complex	3	$175	$200
1940	Helsinki	Silk scarf with Finnish flag and Olympic rings	5	$75	$100
1948	London	Brass cigarette case with Olympic rings, "Olympic Games London 1948"	4	$125	$150
1948	London	Official travel pass for athletes and officials	4	$50	$75
1948	London	Linen scarf with athletes, Olympic rings and legend	4	$75	$100
1948	St. Moritz	Competitor's bib	3	$350	$400
1948	St. Moritz	Cotton handkerchief with ski jumper, Olympic rings over legend in corner	3	$125	$150
1952	Helsinki	Silk handkerchief with flags of competing nations and Olympic rings with date	4	$50	$60
1952	Helsinki	Silk pennant with stadium, Olympic rings, and legend	4	$75	$100
1952	Helsinki	Cotton handkerchief with flags of competing nations, Olympic rings, view of Olympic stadium	5	$75	$100
1952	Helsinki	Large brass matchbox cover	4	$50	$60
1952	Helsinki	Linen scarf with flags of competing nations, stadium, Olympic rings and legend	4	$50	$75

1948, St. Moritz. Cotton handkerchief with ski jumper, Olympic rings over legend in corner, $125-150.

1952, Helsinki. Silk handkerchief with flags of competing nations and Olympic rings, $50-60.

1940, Helsinki. Silk scarf with Finnish flag and Olympic rings, $75-100.

1948, London. Official travel pass for athlete's and officials, $50-75.

Year	City	Description	Rarity	Avg	Nr Mint
1952	Helsinki	Bronze torch relay plaque with Helsinki flame logo	5	$75	$100
1952	Helsinki	Metal ashtray with legend around edge & Olympic flag in center	5	$25	$35
1952	Helsinki	Small enameled brass matchbox cover	4	$45	$55
1952	Helsinki	Small brass matchbox cover	4	$35	$45
1952	Oslo	Silk patch with round games logo	4	$50	$75
1952	Oslo	Small cloth pennant with skier over Norwegian flag, Olympic rings and legend	3	$75	$100
1952	Oslo	Silk patch with games logo over legend	4	$50	$75
1952	Oslo	Competitor's bib	3	$350	$400
1952	Oslo	Cotton handkerchief with sports graphics & official logo	3	$75	$100
1952	Oslo	Ceramic tile depicting ski jumper over Olympic rings	4	$225	$250
1956	Cortina	Competitor's bib	3	$325	$375
1956	Melbourne	Cup and saucer in china with games logo on each	4	$75	$100
1956	Melbourne	Plastic ashtray with Olympic rings & torch over Australia	5	$25	$35
1956	Melbourne	Metal cookie container with overview of main stadium on lid	5	$50	$75
1956	Melbourne	Souvenir glass with games logo	4	$75	$85
1956	Melbourne	Official U.S. team patch	4	$35	$50

1952, Oslo. Silk patch with round games logo, $50-75.

1952, Helsinki. Silk pennant with stadium, Olympic rings, and legend, $75-100.

1952, Oslo. Small cloth pennant with skier over Norwegian flag, Olympic rings and legend, $75-100.

1952, Oslo. Silk patch with games logo over legend, $50-75.

1956, Melbourne. Official U.S. team patch, $35-50.

Year	City	Description	Rarity	Avg	Nr Mint
1956	Melbourne	Felt pennant with Olympic flame over Australia with legend	4	$50	$75
1956	Stockholm	Brass platter with games logo in center	4	$300	$325
1956	Stockholm	Glass vase with etched games logo	4	$300	$325
1960	Rome	Silk scarf with Olympic torch over map of Italy and Greece surrounded by athletes	4	$75	$100
1960	Rome	Official U.S. team patch	4	$35	$50
1960	Rome	Alabaster-like green glass ashtray with games logo	4	$70	$80
1960	Squaw Valley	Cobalt blue shot glass with Olympic rings and legend	4	$35	$45
1960	Squaw Valley	Glass paperweight with skier design in center	5	$50	$60
1960	Squaw Valley	Souvenir patch with official games logo	4	$20	$25
1960	Squaw Valley	Official U.S. team patch	3	$35	$55
1960	Squaw Valley	Acetate scarf with games logo, skier, venues, and legend	4	$100	$125
1960	Squaw Valley	Silver plated spoon with games logo at top	4	$75	$90
1960	Squaw Valley	Small blue felt pennant with overview of Olympic arena and logo with legend	4	$50	$75
1960	Squaw Valley	Large felt pennant with skier & legend	4	$100	$125
1960	Squaw Valley	Commemorative cobalt blue shot glass	4	$35	$45
1960	Squaw Valley	Competitor's bib	3	$300	$350
1960	Squaw Valley	Metal ashtray with embossed games logo	4	$45	$55
1960	Squaw Valley	Ceramic ashtray with winter scene, Olympic rings in center	5	$40	$50
1960	Squaw Valley	Ceramic candy dish with Olympic rings, skier	5	$55	$65
1960	Squaw Valley	Souvenir patch with Olympic torch, Olympic rings and legend	4	$25	$35

1960, Rome. Official U.S. team patch, $35-50.

1960, Rome. Silk scarf with Olympic torch over map of Italy and Greece surrounded by athletes, $75-100.

1960, Rome. Alabaster-like green glass ashtray with games logo, $70-80.

1960, Squaw Valley. Ceramic ashtray with winter scene, Olympic rings in center, $40-50.

1960, Squaw Valley. Ceramic candy dish with Olympic rings, skier, $55-65.

1960, Squaw Valley. Official U.S. team patch, $35-55.

1960, Squaw Valley. Silver-plated spoon with games logo at top, $75-90.

1960, Squaw Valley. Cobalt blue shot glass with Olympic rings and legend, $35-45.

1960, Squaw Valley. Souvenir patch with Olympic torch, Olympic rings and legend, $25-35.

1960, Squaw Valley. Small blue felt pennant with overview of Olympic arena and logo with legend, $50-75.

Year	City	Description	Rarity	Avg	Nr Mint
1960	Squaw Valley	Glass ashtray with games logo applied to bottom	5	$50	$65
1964	Innsbruck	Competitor's bib	3	$225	$275
1964	Innsbruck	Silk scarf with large official logo in center	4	$75	$100
1964	Tokyo	Enameled chrome lighter with games logo	4	$75	$90
1964	Tokyo	Gold plated metal sake cup with legend and rings	5	$50	$60
1964	Tokyo	Silk scarf with rising sun and legend in center surround by athletes in various sports	5	$50	$60
1964	Tokyo	Official U.S. team patch	4	$35	$50
1964	Tokyo	Souvenir logo patch	5	$10	$15
1968	Grenoble	Souvenir gray ceramic mug with games logo in metal	4	$40	$50
1968	Grenoble	Competitor's bib	3	$225	$275
1968	Grenoble	Blue souvenir patch of logo	5	$15	$20
1968	Grenoble	Porcelain plate with blue graphic of skier & geometric patterns with official logo on rim	4	$45	$55
1968	Grenoble	Aluminum ashtray with games logo in center	5	$35	$45
1968	Grenoble	Acetate scarf with large official logo in center	4	$75	$100
1968	Grenoble	ABC Television patch	3	$100	$125
1968	Mexico City	Official U.S. team patch	4	$35	$50
1968	Mexico City	Media armband	4	$60	$75

1968, Grenoble. ABC Television patch, $100-125.

1968, Grenoble. Aluminum ashtray with games logo in center, $35-45.

1964, Tokyo. Souvenir logo patch, $10-15.

1964, Tokyo. Enameled chrome lighter with games logo, $75-90.

1968, Mexico City. Media armband, $60-75.

Year	City	Description	Rarity	Avg	Nr Mint
1972	Munich	Porcelain plate depicting Olympic cauldron with legend around edge	5	$45	$55
1972	Munich	Official U.S. team patch	4	$35	$50
1972	Munich	Official Swedish team patch	4	$20	$25
1972	Munich	Steel lighter with games logo on one side	5	$60	$75
1972	Sapporo	Gold plated metal sake cup with legend	4	$55	$65
1972	Sapporo	Competitor's bib	3	$225	$275
1976	Innsbruck	Red plastic and metal lighter with games logo on one side	4	$45	$55
1976	Innsbruck	Official competition hockey puck with games logo	3	$125	$150
1976	Innsbruck	Competitor's bib	3	$175	$200
1976	Innsbruck	Mascot pendant in brass with chain	3	$45	$65

1972, Munich. Steel lighter with games logo on one side, $60-75.

1972, Munich. Official Swedish team patch, $20-25.

1976, Innsbruck. Competitor's bib, $175-200.

1972, Munich. Official U.S. team patch, $35-50.

1976, Innsbruck. Mascot pendant in brass with chain, $45-65.

Year	City	Description	Rarity	Avg	Nr Mint
1976	Innsbruck	Round, multifaceted paperweight in glass by Saworoski, with games logo	4	$75	$100
1976	Innsbruck	Square paperweight in glass with games logo at bottom	4	$50	$75
1976	Montreal	Large size logo flag	4	$110	$125
1976	Montreal	Medium size logo flag	4	$80	$95
1976	Montreal	Metal lighter with games logo applied to one side	5	$30	$35
1976	Montreal	Porcelain plate depicting Olympic cauldron with legend around edge	5	$45	$55
1976	Montreal	Official Sweden team patch	4	$20	$25
1976	Montreal	Official U.S. team patch	4	$35	$50
1980	Lake Placid	Medium size logo flag	4	$80	$95
1980	Lake Placid	Chrome lighter with games logo	4	$45	$55
1980	Lake Placid	Souvenir patch of logo in blue	5	$5	$7
1980	Lake Placid	Large size logo flag	4	$110	$125
1980	Lake Placid	Competitor's bib	3	$175	$200
1980	Lake Placid	Souvenir patch of logo in color	5	$5	$7
1980	Lake Placid	Pewter mug with official logo	5	$10	$15
1980	Lake Placid	Official U.S. team ring	3	$500	$600
1980	Lake Placid	Official organizing committee medal	4	$75	$100
1980	Lake Placid	Souvenir hockey puck with mascot	5	$25	$35
1980	Lake Placid	Souvenir hockey puck with games logo	5	$25	$35
1980	Lake Placid	Glass paperweight with engraved plate and mascot applied	5	$35	$45
1980	Lake Placid	Glass paperweight with engraved plate and games logo applied	5	$35	$45
1980	Lake Placid	Official organizing committee patch	3	$75	$100
1980	Lake Placid	Official U.S. team patch	3	$50	$75

1976, Montreal. Metal lighter with games logo applied to one side. $30-35.

1976, Montreal. Official Sweden team patch, $20-25.

1976, Innsbruck. Official competition hockey puck with games logo, $125-150.

1976, Innsbruck. Square paperweight in glass with games logo at bottom, $50-75.

1980, Lake Placid. Chrome lighter with games logo, $45-55.

1980, Lake Placid. Glass paperweight with engraved plate and mascot applied, $35-45.

1980, Lake Placid. Official U.S. team patch, $50-75.

1980, Lake Placid. Official organizing committee medal, $75-100.

1980, Lake Placid. Official U.S. team ring, $500-600.

1980, Lake Placid. Official organizing committee patch, $75-100.

1980, Lake Placid. Pewter mug with official logo, $10-15.

Year	City	Description	Rarity	Avg	Nr Mint
1980	Moscow	Souvenir logo patch	5	$5	$10
1980	Moscow	Acetate scarf with games mascot	5	$40	$50
1980	Moscow	Zenit 35mm SLR camera with games logo	4	$75	$100
1980	Moscow	Commemorative Soviet made watch with games logo	4	$75	$100
1980	Moscow	Porcelain cup and saucer with games logo	5	$50	$75
1980	Moscow	Porcelain plate depicting Olympic cauldron with legend around edge	5	$45	$55
1984	Los Angeles	Commemorative Waterford crystal Olympic medallion	5	$40	$50
1984	Los Angeles	Official U.S. team patch	4	$35	$50
1984	Los Angeles	Porcelain plate depicting official logo	5	$35	$45
1984	Los Angeles	Official competition baseball with games logo	4	$50	$75
1984	Los Angeles	"Official Commemorative Ball" baseball with games logo	5	$20	$25
1984	Los Angeles	Competitor's number	3	$40	$50
1984	Los Angeles	Porcelain plate depicting Olympic cauldron with legend around edge	4	$75	$85

1980, Lake Placid. Souvenir patch of logo in blue, $5-7.

1980, Lake Placid. Souvenir patch of logo in color, $5-7.

1980, Lake Placid. Souvenir hockey puck with games logo, $25-35.

1980, Moscow. Souvenir logo patch, $5-10.

1980, Lake Placid. Souvenir hockey puck with mascot, $25-35.

1984, Lcs Angeles. Competitor's number, $40-50.

Year	City	Description	Rarity	Avg	Nr Mint
1984	Los Angeles	Medium size logo flag	5	$50	$75
1984	Sarajevo	Medium size logo flag	4	$125	$150
1984	Sarajevo	Competitor's bib	4	$150	$175
1984	Sarajevo	Glass candlestick by Orrefors, in the shape of Olympic cauldron with Olympic rings	5	$25	$30
1984	Sarajevo	Official competition hockey puck with games logo	3	$150	$175
1984	Sarajevo	Official U.S. team patch	4	$35	$50
1984	Sarajevo /Los Angeles	Official U.S. team watch	3	$125	$150

1984, Los Angeles. Official competition baseball with games logo, $50-75.

1984, Sarajevo. Official U.S. team patch, $35-50.

1984, Sarajevo/Los Angeles. Official U.S. team watch, $125-150.

1984, Los Angeles. Official U.S. team patch, $35-50.

1984 Sarajevo. Official competition hockey puck with games logo, $150-175.

1988, Seoul. Official competition baseball with games logo, $75-100.

Year	City	Description	Rarity	Avg	Nr Mint
1988	Calgary	Competitor's bib	4	$150	$175
1988	Calgary	Souvenir hockey puck with games logo	5	$25	$35
1988	Seoul	Official competition baseball with games logo	3	$75	$100
1988	Seoul	Porcelain plate depicting Olympic cauldron with legend around edge	5	$45	$55
1988	Seoul	Souvenir baseball with multi-colored logo	4	$35	$50
1988	Seoul	Competitor's number	3	$40	$50
1992	Albertville	Glass medallion by Lalique, of figure skater	4	$100	$125
1992	Albertville	Official competition hockey puck with games logo	3	$125	$150
1992	Albertville	Glass medallion by Lalique, of skier	4	$100	$125
1992	Albertville	Souvenir hockey puck with games logo	5	$40	$50
1992	Albertville	Souvenir hockey puck with mascot	5	$40	$50

1992, Albertville. Official competition hockey puck with games logo, $125-150.

1992, Albertville. Glass medallion by Lalique, similar to prize medal, $125-150.

1992, Albertville. Souvenir phone cards, $10-15.

1992, Albertville. Official Canadian team patch with games logo and team logo, $15-20.

1992, Barcelona. Competitor's number, $40-50.

Year	City	Description	Rarity	Avg	Nr Mint
1992	Albertville	Glass medallion by Lalique, similar to prize medal	4	$125	$150
1992	Albertville	Official Canadian team patch with games logo and team logo	5	$15	$20
1992	Albertville	Souvenir phone cards	4	$10	$15
1992	Albertville	Competitor's bib	4	$150	$175
1992	Barcelona	Official Puerto Rico team patch	5	$15	$20
1992	Barcelona	Watch with games logo given to official media	4	$40	$50
1992	Barcelona	Competitor's number	3	$40	$50
1992	Barcelona	Seiko U.S. Olympic team commemorative watch	5	$50	$75
1994	Lillehammer	Official U.S. team patch	5	$20	$25
1994	Lillehammer	Competitor's bib	4	$150	$175
1996	Atlanta	Official competition baseball with games logo	4	$75	$100
1996	Atlanta	Round paperweight in glass with pewter rim and games logo	5	$10	$15
1996	Atlanta	Competitor's number	4	$15	$20
1998	Nagano	Souvenir U.S. team patch	5	$15	$20
1998	Nagano	Official Russian team medal	4	$75	$100
1998	Nagano	Porcelain plate depicting snowlet mascots	5	$35	$45
1998	Nagano	Competitor's bib	4	$150	$175
1998	Nagano	Souvenir hockey puck with games logo	5	$25	$30
1998	Nagano	Official competition hockey puck with games logo	3	$100	$125
2000	Sydney	Official competition baseball with games logo	4	$50	$75
2000	Sydney	Competitor's number	4	$15	$20
2000	Sydney	Souvenir baseball with multi-color games logo	5	$10	$15

1996, Atlanta. Official competition baseball with games logo, $75-100.

1998, Nagano. Official competition hockey puck with games logo, $100-125.

1998, Nagano. Official Russian team medal, $75-125.

1994, Lillehammer. Official U.S. team patch, $20-25.

1996, Atlanta. Competitor's number, $15-20.

2000, Sydney. Souvenir baseball with multi-color games logo, $10-15.

Bibliography

Bushing, David. *Sports Equipment Price Guide "A Century of Sports Equipment from 1860 – 1960."* Iola, Wisconsin: Krause Publications, 1995.

Greensfelder, Jim, Vorontsov, Oleg, and Lally, Jim. *Olympic Medals A Reference Guide.* Madrid, Spain: Luminar, S.L. 1968.

Lattimer, George M. *III Olympic Winter Games Lake Placid 1932*. III Olympic Winter Games Committee, 1932.

1896-1984, Olympism Through Posters. International Olympic Committee, 1983.

Xth Olympiad Los Angeles 1932, Official Report, Xth Olympiade Committee of the Games of Los Angeles, U.S.A. 1932, LTD., 1933.